One Man's
WIGSTON

One Man's
WIGSTON

*Sixty Years' Recollections of
Everyday Life in Wigston Magna*

O . D . Lucas

SUTTON PUBLISHING
LEICESTERSHIRE MUSEUMS, ARTS AND RECORDS SERVICE

First published in the United Kingdom in 1993 by
Leicestershire Museums, Arts and Records Service

Managed by Alan Sutton Publishing Ltd, an imprint of
Sutton Publishing Limited
Phoenix Mill · Thrupp · Stroud · Gloucestershire GL5 2BU

Reprinted in 2000

Leicestershire Museums, Arts & Records Service publication no. 124

A catalogue record for this book is available from the British Library

ISBN 0–7509–0457–7

Typeset in 12/13 Garamond.
Typesetting and origination by
Sutton Publishing Limited.
Printed in Great Britain by
Redwood Books,
Trowbridge, Wiltshire.

Contents

Foreword

To anyone with even the faintest interest in local history, the name Wigston Magna strikes a familiar note. In 1957 the late W G Hoskins wrote *The Midland Peasant*, a detailed study of the history of Wigston Magna from its beginnings, as an Anglian settlement of the sixth century, until 1900.

In this classic of local history, Hoskins aimed to demonstrate the continuity in the economy and life of the free peasantry in Wigston (and many other Midland villages) over 1,500 years. By implication, the late nineteenth century was seen as a watershed in this story, with rapid population increase and industrialisation destroying, or at least submerging Wigston's agrarian, village culture.

Although far more humble in purpose, *One Man's Wigston* complements *The Midland Peasant* in two ways. Firstly, it refutes Hoskins' implied despondency that agrarian village culture in Wigston was dead by the turn of the century. Mr Lucas gives us very many keenly observed character studies of Wigstonians which could only be possible in a community still possessing considerable homogeneity and dependence upon agricultural resources and methods of production.

Secondly, we soon realise that the Wigston of Mr Lucas' childhood and adolescence is very different to the Wigston of the 1990s. The close integration of domestic life, work and the community with each other and with the agricultural year no longer exists. He therefore shows that although Midland peasant culture was declining by the Victorian period, its final death has come about only very recently.

But there is much more to this book than its complementing academic historical writing. Mr Lucas has eschewed accounts of administrative history or detailed topographical description to concentrate on the *people* of Wigston Magna. The result is greatly subjective, but very rich in information about the human condition. The author has been blessed with a sharp eye for detail, a keen ear for a good story and a long memory, and he has put these to very good use. He presents a huge cast of village characters – the sinners as well as the saints – and shows them interacting with each other and with their home environment.

Ironically, publications such as this which, by comparison with the present, highlight the fragmentation of community spirit are also positive aids to promoting it. Too often the rich reminiscences of long-standing villagers are considered as anachronistic and hostile to present-day newcomers. Such critiscisms fail to see how these mines of local information, gossip and storytelling provide some of the wherewithal for the newcomers to understand their adopted environment as well as pass on a body of common knowledge to share with the more established residents. Furthermore, a close reading of this text will show that many of the "well established" Wigston families have only been resident in the village for two or three generations and were themselves once newcomers.

We should also be very grateful to Mr Lucas for realising the importance of the changes he has witnessed over the past 60 or so years, and his perseverence in committing them to paper for the benefit of us all. The recent past is notoriously difficult to view rationally and the mundane things of work and play very easy to disregard. Often, it is only by trying to make sense of these ordinary things in our own lives that we gain a better insight into the greater movements of history.

Steph Mastoris, The Harborough Museum
Leicestershire Museums, Arts & Records Service

The Leicestershire Remembered series

This book is the first in a projected series by Leicestershire Museums, Arts & Records Service which will publish personal reminiscences by the people of Leicestershire and Rutland.

When so much of the work of Leicestershire Museums is directed at the preservation and interpretation of artefacts relating to everyday life in the county, it seems very fitting that the memories of the people who used such items are also recorded. Frequently, this has taken the form of recorded interviews, and the Service now has several hundreds of hours of taped conversations with many local people. A few museum publications have already drawn upon this material, perhaps the most notable being *Cap and Apron: an Oral History of Domestic Service in the Shires, 1880-1950*, by Samuel Mullins and Gareth Griffiths (1986).

Often, however, people prefer to write down their memories and the success of the "As I Remember It" series produced by Leicestershire Libraries is a glowing testimony of this. The "Leicestershire Remembered" series will aim to complement these small anthologies by publishing more lengthy accounts of life in the past which have a distinct bearing on the present.

Introduction

I have a passionate and lifelong interest in the history of Great Wigston. Born at number ten Bell Street, on 13 March 1929, I have never been away from the town for more than three weeks at any one time, and then only on holidays.

Some time ago, while watching the television, I was interested to hear the views of Fred Archer, a character whose village population had soared from 350 to 650 souls. "The village has grown so much I no longer know everybody!" he said. His words had an impact on me.

To walk in Bell Street and see a great mass of people, yet only rarely recognise a familiar face saddens me. The buildings which held such pleasant memories are gone. The fields are disappearing beneath a great tide of bricks and mortar. The village people are swamped by a massive influx of new arrivals. The village has become a town. Some call it "progress", the "march of time" and say that "there is nothing you can do about it!" The clichés are trotted out relentlessly.

There is one thing that I am determined to do about it – the village, its traditions and its characters shall not pass away unnoticed. During my life I have been privileged to meet many great characters and I have heard them tell their stories, listened enthralled as they spun their yarns. Stories by Wigstonians (some now long dead) may still live on, by being faithfully remembered and recorded here.

These reminiscences were started almost ten years ago and in the intervening time have steadily grown. I would like to record my thanks to the late Jean Valman (née Bass), who laboriously and lovingly worked to interpret my illegible handwritten and taped memories. Also to Steph Mastoris, Keeper of the Harborough Museum (Leicestershire Museums), and his one-time assistant, Adrian Green, who gave considerable assistance in reorganising and editing my random memories.

Unless otherwise stated, the photographs in this book are from my own collection, and I am most grateful to the many people who have kindly given or loaned me these photographs over the years.

Last, but by no means least, thanks to Jean, an Oadby lass who married me and still wonders what has happened !

Duncan Lucas, Wigston Magna, January 1993

The author, with his horse, "Betsy", 1952.

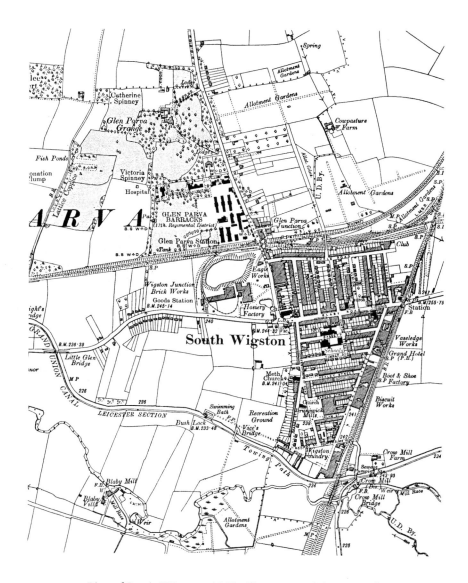

Plan of South Wigston, 1931. (Crown copyright reserved)

Plan of Wigston Magna, 1930. (Crown copyright reserved)

Chapter One

Around Wigston, starting at No. 10 Bell Street

Number ten, Bell Street, Wigston Magna in the County of Leicestershire was my birthplace and from there runs this tale. So let's take a journey around the village (the maps on pages 14 and 15 will help show the way).

BELL STREET AND LEICESTER ROAD

In the very early 1930s Bell Street was the main street of Wigston, but still quiet enough for a small child to play in. The street was a community in its own right in those days. Mrs Garforth kept the fish and chip shop at the bottom of the street opposite "Forryan's Corner" – at the west end of Bell Street where Leicester Road and Long Street meet. On Forryan's Corner was the home of the Forryan clan, of which I am an offshoot. There was a butcher's shop with an attached slaughter house on one side and a house on the other. On the corner which curved round into Leicester Road were cow sheds, then pig sties and on Leicester Road proper was the barn, fasting pens, orchard and garden. It is strange to stand on the car park at the rear of the present shops and remember how, as a child, I saw sheep grazing there.

Cousin Willie Forryan and I played for many happy hours on Bell Street corner (alias Ball Dyke). We used to sit on a trap in the cart shed

Bell Street, from "Forryan's Corner", about 1900.

at the end of the house and shout across the road "Melias mouldy cheeses", until Mr Glover the manager of Melias grocery shop chased us off. Cattle were slaughtered there up until the war and what an event that was for us children!

Next to Billy Cox's, at the junction of Long Street and Leicester Road, was King's the chemist. Mr King was a very upright gentleman, much respected by us children. People used to go to him for their teeth extractions. He was very nervous and hated the job. Uncle Cecil, one of my Forryan uncles, told me that when he first entered into practice as a chemist in Leicester, he had all of Mr King's dentist's kit. Uncle also told that when he was a lad Mr King would pull down the blind at his Chemist's shop when about to extract someone's teeth. As soon as they saw the blind pulled down, the locals gathered around to hear the screams and yells from the patient having teeth seen to without any anaesthetic!

I have some of the old boxes with their glass knobs in which Mr King used to keep various medicines in his shop. His wife, formerly Stella

Bell Street, looking east, about 1935.

Laundon, lived in Bull Head Street. I have also a box label of Mr King's advertising "Teeth Extractions and Chemist". He ceased extracting teeth in the 1920s.

Next door but one to King's was the Post Office and the Co-op was between the two – all on Long Street. The Postmaster at that time was named Mr Way, a very quiet gentleman. I don't know if it is my memory which makes everyone seem so quiet and respectable, but then it was a different age with different attitudes and I was very young.

Before Mr Way, Shipps ran the Post Office at the top of Bell Street. Mr Wilford, a farmer, had a son called Vin. He told the tale that when they lived up Newton Lane, at the back of Linley's Lodge, which is now Highfield House, they didn't get their post because Mr Shipp the Postmaster did not want to deliver until it was worth his while going that distance. So the Wilfords got everybody they could to send them postcards. Vin chuckled when he recounted how Mr Shipp took his father to task because he read the postcards and one of them said "Hope you are well and that miserable old devil Shipp will deliver this card to you". I believe the post had to go up there daily from there on. I have record of a telegraph machine being installed at Shipps in 1879.

Long Street, looking north, about 1935.

FREDERICK STREET

Next comes Frederick Street, which was originally called Mill Lane. Some years ago I stood talking to Bronx Snowden, one of Wigston's older inhabitants at that time (he was a retired teacher somewhere around 90 years of age and I had many a chat with him and saved a few interesting items in his house from being dumped into the refuse cart for burning). We were standing on the corner of Frederick Street, and I asked Mr Snowden why it was called Mill Lane. He replied "Why lad, George Hassell's dad had a watermill there". I asked where did the water come from – "Out of the ground, there was a tremendous spring down there and it used to run a little mill which he used to run his factory". When a new well was sunk in Holyoak's yard in Bell Street it reduced the pressure of the water and the mill fell out of use. How the name got changed from Mill Lane to Frederick Street, he could not say, but it would appear that a builder Frederick Burgess had something to do with it. The village hall was in Frederick Street and I have heard the tales of my Grandma dancing with my grandfather Forryan there.

Snowdens were needle makers and had a little tiny cottage against their rather tall house which was a Quaker Chapel and, I believe, a school

Leicester Road, looking north, about 1935.

at one time, but built as a Mechanics Institute. This was on The Bank which was the old junction of Oadby Lane (not "Road" as it came to be known), Bull Head Street and Bell Street.

The Shipps were the dominant family, because of the large house with the very prosperous draper's business carried out there. Their old house was once the Bell Inn. This inn was closed down when the Shipps created their business and at the rear was the strict Baptist Chapel. It is said that the doorway of this strict Baptist Chapel was an old doorway from the old Bell Inn – someone with a wry sense of humour pulled a fast one!

Bell Street Infants School once stood on the site today occupied by Sainsbury's. By the side of that school and still in existence is the "jetty" down which as children we used to race our "trolleys" – a vehicle composed of a crude plank on four pram wheels. Today we think skate boarders are mad and dangerous with the recklessness of youth, but careering along those trolleys and their human cargo must have appeared a fearsome sight rushing toward our elders!

The Bell Jetty is an obvious extension of Long Lane and was probably the footpath to Leicester which ran parallel to that road. "Ball Dyke" is the area of Leicester Road from Bell Street, which was once known as

Frederick Street, looking east, 1920s. This street was formerly called Mill Lane, after a Mill powered by spring water.

Ball Dyke Street, to Aylestone Lane. Even today, old Wigstonians still refer to the Ball Dyke as "the village".

William Cox owned land in Aylestone Lane, now the area around the Nautical William. In latter years Mr Wilford was Cox's tenant, and what names his fields had – Lovedays, Franklins, Saltys, The Parlour, Little Meadow, Long Fields, Black Hut Fields, Ladkins, Footroad Field, First and Second Field, Big Brewin. All have disappeared under part of Central Avenue, Holmden Avenue estate and the Industrial estate. It is a great pity that none of the lovely old names were perpetuated as street names, as was done with Wigston Harcourt. For a reason I could never discover, Billy Cox senior used to call my uncle Les "Lasarus"!

I can well remember the old gas lamps used in Wigston for street lights. They had two little chains hanging, one for switching the lamp on and one for switching it off. A man by the name of Mr Gibbs was the lamplighter, he lived on Kings Drive and would ride round on his bike with a small ladder and a pole. On the end of the pole was a hook and a small lighted wick. The hook was used to pull the chain which released the gas and was immediately ignited by the small flame. He used to pop up on his ladder to change the mantles if they were broken. In the morning he would ride round and switch the lamps off. It seems a far off age seeing the sodium lights of today come on and go off untouched by human hand, but they should make us realise the simply fantastic improvements we have seen over a fairly short period. When the gas industry was nationalised after the war, it was said the gas ran through holes in the ground, so ancient were the gas pipes of Wigston that they had disintegrated.

There was an elderly lady named Mrs Mawby, who lived in Bull Head Street opposite the factory owned by Broughtons in those days. She protested most vigorously when it was suggested that she should have electricity. "How am I going to keep my house warm?" she demanded. It must be remembered that the gas gave off warmth as well as light. Mrs Mawby had a picture and medals in a frame over her mantlepiece. I believe the frame and the "regret" letter from the War Office commemorated her son lost in the terrible First World War. Many homes had this tragic display.

JUNCTION ROAD AND BURGESS STREET

Frederick Street and Burgess Street have Junction Road linking them. These were laid out by Frederick Burgess who lived at The Grange. I believe he also did the excavation of the sandpits in the front. I am told that Stone Age tools were found at this pit and were sold, unfortunately, for only a very nominal sum by the owners and a little bit of evidence of old Wigston has disappeared because of this.

The Junction Road – Burgess Street area like most areas of Wigston has lost all resemblance of its old character. But it was up here in Junction Road at Ellwell's workshop that Jack Mill had a sawmill. He was a veteran of the First World War with one leg. He used to saw his logs and deliver them by pony and trap. He had a wonderful bass voice and as a lad at Chapel I used to love to hear him sing. When I delivered milk in Junction Road I would hear Jack religiously practising.

ST WOLSTAN'S CHURCH

Another shop on Forryan's Corner was run by another very well-loved Wigston character Mrs Proctor. She was a grand old lady who made homemade toffee. During the Second World War she had an extra allowance of sugar to make her wares and how we used to enjoy her homemade toffee. I also used to enjoy her yarns of Old Wigston. One tale she told me was of St Wolstan's Churchyard. She said that when she was a small girl there used to be snowdrops over the wall of the Churchyard and that there were some cottages at the bottom of St Wolstan's Churchyard, noting "You can see there are no graves at this point". Folks said she must be daft, who would have built houses there?

But research proved her right. Records show that money was left to build almshouses at the bottom of the Churchyard in 1682. The Churchyard was reused for burials between the time that All Saints' yard was closed and the Wharf Road (Welford Road) cemetery was opened.

A look around the church and churchyard is worthwhile. I hope the gravestones will be left to show the old family groups, the Shipps, Forryans, Goodwins and other families. The church has a leper window in the tower. It was once used as a stable and a store, became a ruin, was resuscitated as a school room and used for the early meetings of the

Aerial view of All Saints' Church, looking south, about 1950. On the left are some of the cottages at the top of Newgate End, and the village pinfold. Immediately behind the church tower is Rectory Farmhouse, destroyed by a soulless Wigston Urban District Council.

Congregational church (now in a beautiful building in Long Street, but renamed The United Reform church).

On the Wigston/Oadby border, a parson tipped over in his trap and was killed. This bit of road became known as "Parson's Bend" and retained that name for many years, though there are few there today who would remember it.

We now move south through Bull Head Street to the Newton Lane and Welford Road area.

BULL HEAD STREET

When the old cruck cottages adjacent to the Bull's Head Inn were knocked down by Ted Fisher, I had some of the old timbers which are now in my own museum. Others went to Kibworth and were built into the front of a house to replace a porch. This had been built in the reign of Henry VII, the victor of Bosworth Field, and the owner wanted authentic timbers. So a bit of old Wigston lives still at the front of an old house at Kibworth.

Bull Head Street, looking south, about 1935.

NEWTON LANE

Mr Ludlam a farmer and shopkeeper told me of a workhouse up Newton Lane. A "slang" or narrow strip of land which existed on the right hand side of the road near Glebe Farm entrance was the site of a clash between some hosiery (or framework) knitters and the militia in the nineteenth century – a strike was on and tempers were frayed.

The people of old selected their village sites because of the shallow water available. At the back of "Gravel Hole", a field in Newton Lane, there is a well six feet deep. Water is syphoned from here down to a water trough and has never been known to run dry. The problem occurs when the syphon gets air locked and after much sucking, cursing and blowing the air lock is removed and the water flows again. The syphon is controlled at its trough by a ball cock.

There are still remains of allotments on one side of the Welford Road. There is Cottage Road which stands on the Stanhope allotment. I thought that Stanhope was taken from Stanhope Rolleston, the South Wigston Squire, but it was not, the name is a corruption of the Standup Sick Club (I am grateful to Mrs Goodwin, née Wignall, for giving me this information).

Moat Street, looking west, 1908. On the left are Diamond Cottages.

MOAT STREET

There was amongst the names of Wigston, Barrack Yard which was at the side of Sewell's shop in Moat Street. The old frame knitters' factory is still used at the rear, but the Barrack Yard sign has gone. Barrack Yard was near the pinfold which Mr Bale used for the name of his house opposite Newgate End. A pinfold is where straying cattle were kept until reclaimed and a fine paid by their owners. It was said that if the straying animal was female and in milk, it was milked out before being returned to the owner, be it sheep, goat or cow, no mention was made of pig or pigeon. A seat on the corner of Newgate End is on the Pinfold site.

ALL SAINTS' CHURCH

The old Rectory farmhouse and buildings which appeared to be almost wrapped around the Church have long gone. I believe the loss of the beautiful old Rectory farmhouse with its iron hard bricks is another terrible indictment of our local authority as it was destroyed on their recommendation. If you want to see a little of the old Rectory farmhouse, you must go to Donington le Heath Manorhouse. A small staircase that came from this house has been re-erected there.

NEWGATE END

If we make our way back again to Newgate End, a large house used to stand on the site of the present Council yard. The last person to live there was Mr Fred Ashbridge, the then Sanitary Inspector. The house was once an asylum or hospital. Whether it housed mentally or phyisically sick I am not quite sure. The commercial directory of 1843 refers to it as an Asylum. There also used to be quite a lot of terraced cottages in Newgate End. Newgate End was new in the time of King Edward I.

The oldest house in Wigston and one of the first to be built in brick is dated 1691. It stands back from the road on the left hand side of Newgate End, if you enter from Moat Street. An extra third storey was built on at some time, the old house had dormer windows in the roof. The Pochin family originally had the house built. The Pochins were related to the Pochins of Barkby Hall – one of the oldest families in the county. Pochin was Puchin in Wigston.

Next door to this house is a small piece of ground which once contained several cottages. Two dear old ladies by the name of Davenport once lived in one of these cottages. They moved on to Davenport Road and were thrilled when they were introduced to Colonel Pen Lloyd, the Chairman of the Leicestershire County Council at the time when he attended some ceremony in Davenport Road. He asked them if the road was named after them, they said regretfully not them personally, but presumably after the family.

Next door lived the Freckingham family. When I was a schoolboy their father was Governor or Manager of the Old National School in Long Street. I remember "Daddy" Hanford our teacher rapping his desk sharply and ordering us to rise in respect, as this rather portly gentleman carrying a bowler hat walked through our classroom. When he had gone we were told "That, boys and girls, is Mr Freckingham – one of the Managers of the school".

Sports grounds seem to have abounded in old Wigston. There were two circular flat areas on the bank overlooking the old Wash Pit in Newgate End where we used to play cricket. Rumour had it that these were the sites of windmills, but they were probably stack bags or bases for hay or corn stacks. The Primitive Methodist Chapel had a cricket ground on Welford Road opposite the cemetery, and although now it is a football pitch we still refer to it as the cricket ground. Two Steeples had their sports ground at the top end of where Northfield Avenue now is. Wigston Fields Football Club started on Shackerdale Farm and although they are now at Glen Parva, still retain their original name. Wigston Albion used to play on the ground at the rear of the old engine sheds... one can go on adding!

The first playing field was leased from Wiggeston Hospital, on a site between Welford Road, Moat Street and Hosswell Lane.

BUSHLOE END

There is an old house in Bushloe End opposite to the British Legion which was saved from demolition. The house consists of a shop with a workroom built over it. No longer operative as a shop there are still part of its fittings. The house was a cosy little cottage which until 1986 was kept beautifully by the occupant, Miss Carter. At the rear is a cobbled yard which contains the *pièce de résistance*, a framework knitters shop with frames still in working condition. There are various interesting pieces of bric-a-brac and a partly made glove on the hand

28

Bushloe End, about 1990. This master hosier's house with its associated frameshop (seen on the right) have now been preserved as the Wigston Framework Knitters Museum.

looms. These buildings have been preserved by the tireless work of the Wigston Framework Knitters Museum Trust and is now open for the public to enjoy.

The garden itself is a beautiful higgledy-piggledy old English garden. Miss Carter did say to me that as a landscaper, "You must think my garden's a mess". I said, "I think it is adorable". When you enter here you are stepping back into a bygone age. I do trust that this property can be preserved for all time in the loveable state that it is today

Next door to this attractive house is the Plough public house. Standing near the church, it probably takes its name from the village plough which was kept in the church porch.

A magnificent chestnut still stands on the corner of Launceston Road and Bushloe End. The latter was one of the most respectable roads in Wigston with Bushloe House on the right where Owstons, the Solicitors lived. As a child I can remember stopping at the gate to the drive to let a car come by and my mother saying "That is Miss Owston — hat off!"

Heatherly House, about 1930. Now demolished. The site is part of the college of further education.

When the family died out the house was purchased by Mr Gunning, the then Town Clerk. Through Mr Gunning's instigation it became the Council Offices. The house itself is a new mansion wrapped around an old farmhouse. The work at Bushloe House is magnificent indeed, anyone entering the offices prepared to spare a few moments to look at the wonderful lock on the door or look up the stairs at the window and ceiling above the stairs, will be rewarded by a sense of this lovely house. Much of the external beauty of the house is now obscured by a modern office block totally devoid of character.

The Owstons were served with meat by the Forryans and sometimes it was delivered by Ernie Forryan. He would take the new meat down into the cellar and bring up the meat he had delivered the previous week. They never ate the meat until it had been hung a week. By the same token it was reckoned not to eat a hare until the farmer had caught (coursed) the next one. My Uncle Ernie met his wife Jesse when she was in service with the Owstons.

STATION ROAD

Further down Station Road was the house called "Heatherley". The College of Further Education now occupies the site. The house was always mysterious, the blinds were always drawn and an elderly gentleman used to come out and get on his bike. He always wore a tweed cap, tweed suit with plus-fours. He had, I remember, a peculiar way of mounting his bike. He would push it along, jump and put one foot on a step beside the back wheel, and then the other foot on the other side, then slip over onto the saddle. It was a work of art!

One slip and it could have been painful, but I never witnessed that!

Below Heatherley was "Tenrow" and as the name suggests it was a row of ten small cottages, on the other side of the road was "Abingdon". Abingdon House and Thomas Ingram formed quite a focal point of Wigston. The railway came and Mr Ingram got the embankment at the bottom by the railway line planted by the company. My great grandfather,

Wigston Magna station, late 1890s. In 1900 this level crossing was replaced by the Spion Kop embankment and a road bridge. The line of the old road, seen here, may still be traced in front of the Railway Inn.

William Forryan, was a close friend of Thomas Ingram and I am told he helped to plant many of the trees which are now at the peak of their maturity.

Thomas Ingram was a solicitor by profession and a public benefactor, he did a lot of work in the Church and played a considerable part in the restoration of St. Wolstan's Church. Legend has it that when St. Thomas's Church at South Wigston was built, he took such a leading part, that the Church was named St. Thomas's as the Church's way of giving him recognition for his work. There is a plaque to him in All Saint's Church. He lived to be 99 and had promised some really magnificent gifts to the Church to celebrate his 100th birthday. Many times he told his friends that he had outlived William Forryan, who died at the relatively early age of 86.

When Thomas Ingram was in his 90s he became very ill. His Doctors had despaired of saving him with medicines so his butler was sent down to his fantastic wine cellar to fetch some bottles of some special claret. It was kill or cure, and it cured.

To celebrate his return to health he toured the South Coast of England in his landau, quite a feat for a man in his 90s. He gave the South Porch to All Saint's Church. Upon his death his nephew, Revd Mortlock, took over Abingdon and the Town had the use of the grounds whenever a special occasion occurred. The house was originally called Hawthorn Field and I believe Revd Mortlock who came from Abingdon, changed the name.

Abingdon house is still there. When I was a lad there were farm buildings where the Bushloe School Gym stands and these were interesting because in the middle of the farm buildings was the old conduit which had been moved there by Thomas Ingram, the builder of Abingdon, for sentimental reasons. This was demolished as nobody wanted it when the schools were built. I believe the stone plaque is in the care of the Leicestershire Museums. One of the farm buildings had a domed sort of dutch barn roof in which there was quite a fair sized hole. It was said that an old man was cleaning a sort of musket held between his knees. It went off, missing him by a fraction and blowing this hole in the roof which never got repaired.

Uncle Les Forryan told how at the Jubilee of Queen Victoria, there was a monster bonfire at Abingdon. The timber that was used on it was fantastic he said, much of it was new timber, it being so cheap and the event such a worthy one. If one stands at Abingdon and looks out across

Wigston Magna Station at Spion Kop, 1920s.

Aerial view of South Wigston, looking north east, 1930s. In the centre of the picture is the pit of the Wigston Junction Brick & Tile Works, and the furrowed field on the right is now occupied by South Wigston High School.

the fields, although the tip and numerous buildings interrupt the view now, one realises how carefully the sites of these houses were selected to ensure a fine prospect for the occupiers.

SPION KOP RAILWAY BRIDGE

Beyond Abingdon is Spion Kop. The old road crossing the railway is to the right of Spion Kop. There was a level crossing at that point before the bridge was built. Opposite the grounds of Abingdon on which the Guthlaxton College is now built, is a residential area known as "The Orchards". It is said that if the people who owned the Orchards had sold their land to the Railway Company, the locomotive works that are at Derby would have been built at Wigston. What effect that would have had in determining Wigston's future and if Orson Wright (whom I shall mention later), had progressed with his dreams, we can only surmise. The area would certainly have been vastly different to the district we know today.

In the fields immediately across the "rally" bridge (a local contraction of the word "railway") on the south side of the main line to London, is a large pit, it is known locally as "Navvy Pit". It was formed in the 1890s, when the navvies built the bridge – Spion Kop – which links South Wigston to Wigston Magna

I remember watching the race horses, which were to compete on the Leicester Racecourse, being walked from the Dock at the side of Spion Kop where they were unloaded from their horse boxes and walked in a long procession up Station Road, along Bushloe End, Long Street, Bell Street, Oadby Lane and enter the racecourse at the Wigston end of the straight mile. The procession seemed never ending and we used to take great delight when a stroppy one started rearing and bucking. The very small men, stable lads, used to lead them. The racecourse was a mysterious place to us. My mother was quite strict and gambling was taboo, although we were allowed to watch with childlike amazement at these very tall animals, never realising at the time how my life would be affected by horses.

CANAL

Who knows of the old canal unloading dock by Evin's lock South Wigston, where manure used to be brought from the Leicester cowsheds?

A newly calved cow used to be bought and spend its life in a backyard in Leicester. Hay and food were imported for it. It would be milked and the milk sold. When the cow eventually dried up it would be slaughtered in the town. The manure it made was not needed to fertilize the very tiny back garden, so it was brought down to the canal and loaded into barges which brought it and unloaded in this old field. It certainly became very fertile. I grew some wonderful crops of potatoes there. The field was part of the old Rectory Farm which was owned by the Duke of St Albans after the enclosures of 1766. The Duke was a descendant of Nell Gwynne and the result of her affair with Charles II.

Frank Freckingham told me that this field had once a funny name. His father called it "Hanging Hill", to which I replied, "That's why the meadow against the river running down to Crow Mill is called Hanging Meadow". Frank asked how I knew and I replied, "Brian Bilson owns a copy of the land sale of Hanging and Nether Meadow dated 1869". It seemed obvious that a hanging took place sometime in the past on the

South Wigston Station and the level crossing gates on the Blaby Road, 1940s.

hill, though further research showed that Hanging Hill is the Saxon name for the Hill that hung over the valley.

The canals have always been an intriguing place to the locals. Turnover Bridge, which is between Wigston and Newton, is where the towpath changes sides, so the old barge horses were taken over the canal by this bridge and commenced their towing from the other side. This was done because the occupier of Wistow at that time, the Earl of Denbigh, insisted that the towpath was kept away from his house at Wistow. The towpath changes sides again on the other side of Kibworth/Wistow Road.

At Double Rail Lock, which is going back between Kilby Bridge and South Wigston, the footpath crosses at this point over the locks. Rumour has it that an old lady drowned whilst crossing the locks. Double hand rails were then fitted to make this safer. Most of these bridges along here have names and they were usually named after the owners of the land adjoining. We have a bridge just the other side of Crow Mills, Vice's Bridge after the Blaby millers; Crow Mills which is well known from the Crow Mill which stands nearby; Irving's Lock which is at the side of an old unloading bay for manure and night soil; Pochin's Bridge – Putchin's Bridge; then we come to Kilby Bridge Lock which is self explanatory (the last lock keeper was a Mr Mercer); Ellis's Bridge, of the Ellis and Everard family (they had land and delphs near Clifton's Bridge which is adjoining the cart track which Cooks Lane develops into); Tythorn Bridge and then Bumble Bee Lock; adjoining Bumble Bee Lock is Bumble Bee Meadow (what a beautiful name!); Langham Bridge (the Langham family had Tythorn farm for many years and built the chapel at Kilby); and Turnover Bridge and Turnover Lock, which are self explanatory.

We now move north from the edges of South Wigston to Aylestone Lane and West Avenue.

AYLESTONE LANE

There used to be a brick yard in Aylestone Lane at the rear of where the Bostik factory is now off West Avenue. It was a similar sort of clay to that in the South Wigston clay pit and houses in Bell Street were built from it. My mother remembers the drying shed and kiln which stood where Wheatcroft's office now is, it was called Goldhill Lodge.

West Avenue leads into Central Avenue, and then meets Long Street where we return to the heart of old Wigston.

The Navigation Inn, Kilby Bridge, about 1900.

Wigston has been fortunate in having so many footpaths, perhaps the most popular was the one up "Dicks" to the "Meres". Dicks being short for Richard Hassel who lived and farmed at the top right hand side of Mowsley End, making one side of "Apple Pie Corner". This route had three approaches from the village, the first was from Mowsley End and through Sherrin's allotments, the second up Church Nook and finally the entrance by the race course on Oadby Road. These three routes joined up in a big field and continued through to the Mere Lane where one could turn left towards Oadby or right into Newton Lane. The popular one for the Little Hill area was up Newton Lane through the allotments to Cooks Lane, over the railway to the canal where we turn right to Kilby Bridge and the Navigation Inn.

The Horsewell footpath again took us through allotments and another approach from Newgate End joined here carrying on over the railway bridge leaving the "Navvy Pit" on our right. Further on we come to the

Aerial view of Wigston, showing Abington House. Under construction are Central Avenue and Clarke Road on the new estate, April 1947.

"Double Rail" lock, turning left to Kilby Bridge or right to Crow Mills and South Wigston. Incidentally the "Navvy Pit" provided excellent skating for the village in Winter. The Pit was rarely used for fishing or swimming, and to fish one had to have permission from Daniel Johnson, the farmer of that time who was a well known Primitive Methodist and Urban District Councillor. The Johnson farm house is the oldest in the village. Unfortunately Joey Gee's, Charlie Willett's, Albert Shipp's and Hill's farms have all disappeared and the once familiar scene of cows strolling down the road has gone forever.

There was a Dudley Street recorded in the records, but I have yet to find its location. Blunt's Lane may record a Wigston surgeon named Blunt. It took a strong protest from the Civic Society to safeguard the lanes in the recent district plan. I think that the lanes were once built on, especially Blunt's Lane. At the time of the Black Death in the 1340s, this area was probably a plague spot and the houses were either burned or left to rot. The inherent fear of this area was passed on to generations until even my mother and father used to say they shouldn't build in the lanes, although they couldn't really say why.

This route around Wigston can still be walked and I hope these memories will help evoke and preserve some of the former character of the village.

Chapter Two

My Family and some other Wigston Characters

A village's character comes from its inhabitants, so I will now deal with the rich collection of interesting and curious people I have been privileged to know in Wigston.

THE LUCAS FAMILY

From an early age I was steeped in the family history. My father talked to us a lot about life and gave me my sense of local pride. His father, a stone mason, lived in a pleasant cottage in Long Street, but dust and grit in his lungs brought hard times to the family. We were poor but my parents were proud, and pride in our heritage perhaps compensated.

My Grandfather Lucas came from Naseby; he was a stone mason and work on building Glen Parva Barracks brought him to Wigston. He became foreman mason on the Grand Hotel Leicester, with 13 men under him. Many local gravestones have his maker's name in the corner. Grandma Lucas came from a Wigston family named Clarke. She told me just before she died in 1945, that there was some connection between us and Royalty. A lawsuit had in the past ruined the Naseby Lucas family. What was the lawsuit? – I don't know, but one day I'll find out!

My father ("Pop") went to war in 1914, joined up at 17. The whole village went to war. Pop served in 1916 in Ireland and many the tale he

Wigston factory lasses cheering the local lads -"Two Steeples' Boys"- off to fight in the First World War from Glen Parva barracks, 3rd September 1914. On the back of this photograph is recorded one of the songs sung at the send-off: "The Kaiser he went up the hill to see the awful slaughter. He came down without his crown and so he damned well oughter!"

told us of "Airland". Then to France and the trenches and the horror of standing up to the waist in water seeing his mates blown to bits or the futile charge into barbed wire and being shot at. Pop was hit by a bullet which was deflected by his wallet, just missing his heart. We used to play with that wallet and show our mates the bullet hole. He was then taken prisoner by the Germans, but at the end of the war he finally returned to England, safely. After my father courted and married mother, Margaret Louise Forryan, her brothers helped him to start a drapery business at 10 Bell Street in gratitude for his war efforts. Successful for a while, the dreadful slumps of the 1930s forced the business to its knees. He then worked for Two Steeples, the world-renowned Wigston Company, the "Rolls Royce" of woollen garments, mainly vests, pants, etc.

I was the first son following three sisters, with two brothers following me. I attended the Bell Street School at four years old, and moved to All Saints School in Long Street, then to City Boys School, Humberstone

My family at 78 Bull Head Street, about 1956. Pop and my mother sit in
the middle of the front row between my sisters José (left) and Marion
(right). I am standing in the middle of the back row, with my brothers
Andy (left) and Brian (right).

Gate Leicester, during the war years. I left school at 15 to work on the
land -wartime was not a good time for education and by the age of 11 I
was already looking after poultry and rabbits, and grew vegetables. I
received additional education at Wigston Congregational Chapel and
trained in public speaking at Young Farmers Clubs. My father was a
Tory, but my uncle Les was a devoted Liberal. The pattern of my life was
forged.

At 23 I married an Oadby lass, Jean Allen, and was farming on my
own account. We had a son Simon and a daughter Anne. I was first
elected at 28 to the urban district council, and was the youngest
chairman at 34. The farming enterprise diversified into gardens and

My wife, Jean, and our horse, "Betsy", about 1952. This was the last-but-
one working horse in Wigston Magna.

landscaping, and civil engineering. My son and daughter are still in the business, and we now have three grandchildren.

THE FORRYAN FAMILY

Forryan is a name peculiar to Leicestershire and like many highly local names its meaning is obscure. Guppy, in his *Homes of Family Names*, says that it may be an altered form of Frewen, an old distinguished family of Leicestershire and Sussex, but this is highly unlikely. Although I cannot trace the name in Leicestershire back beyond the poll tax return of 1377 (to William Forion of Shenton, about three miles south-west of Market Bosworth), the changes of the name during the subsequent three or four hundred years throw some light on its origin. It seems to be a variant of Fearon and Farren, from the old French *feron*, a smith. Farren is more clearly recognisable as a variant form of Fearon, which in turn is obviously from the old French *feron*, but why the Leicestershire form of the name should have acquired the added syllable – Forion and Forryon in its earliest form is unknown.

Over 400 years ago, the Forryans were localised in two places on the western side of the county – Coton in Market Bosworth and at Burbage, seven miles south-south-east. Although the will of William Foreann of Coton (1546) provides the earliest dated reference, the Burbage branch are probably just as old, as we find them well settled there in 1551, in which year they appear as owners of a 60-acre farm in the village. They remained at Burbage as freeholders during the sixteenth, seventeenth and eighteenth centuries and in the latter century at Sketchley also, a neighbouring hamlet; and there are still Forryans in Burbage today. In the early seventeenth century branches of the family spread to Markfield and Congerstone, where the name changed gradually to Farren by the eighteenth century and also at Coton, where we hear of Thomas Farren in 1691. At Burbage the name remained in its original form of Forryan throughout these centuries, except for a very occasional variant as Farren and it is this change of spelling that furnishes the clue to the origin of the name.

Christian names were adopted by families and were passed from father to son, mother to daughter, occasionally missing a generation. In this case the name William had been in the family since 1377, and the name Goodwin was adopted from the Goodwin family into which the Forryans married.

A branch settled at Wigston Magna in the early years of the last century – about the early 1810s. This was Abraham Forryan who came to Wigston via Newton Harcourt and was born in Burbage. Trade was poor and he saw potential at Wigston.

I have the original agreement that William Forryan signed between Arthur Haynes Esq. and himself for three Closes of land called Simonds Close, Middle Wards and Far Wards, at a rent of £32.15s.6d. per annum. This land was where Willow Park Drive and Carlton Drive now stand. I remember the first and second fields as the remains of this plot and the tale of the great drought of 1863 or 1868, when a cart load and a trolley load of hay was the total crop from the 10 acres. Branches were cut from the trees as cattle feed. A mouse could be seen on the ground in the grass so sparse were the blades. Shades of the 1976 drought!

There is mention of an ancient hedgerow on the land. If this was ancient in 1856 the hedge would have been from pre-enclosure days. Perhaps it was a boundary hedge?

Perhaps an enclosure before the open fields in general were enclosed?

I remember in the top corner near Northfields Avenue cursing when we broke a mowing machine on a very awkward bank, perhaps this was it!

Professor Hoskins makes reference to individual enclosures in his book, *The Midland Peasant*, and mentions a court action by Henry White and Richard and William Boulter, dated 1634, over an area of land which had been enclosed and this could have been the site.

By early this century, the Forryan family consisted of Ernest William who became a butcher, Cecil Andrew who became a chemist, Arnold a farmer, Herbert who became a grocer in Nottingham, and Leslie Hedges another farmer (Hedges in this case being his mother's maiden name, from Wytham near Oxford). The usage of the mother's family surname is another old custom being discontinued. My sister José was christened José "Forryan" Lucas, as my mother had despaired of having a son, so sister José got the traditional maiden name, but nature fooled mother, she then had three sons! Edwin Forryan Broughton now lives at Arnesby and is part Forryan, hence his middle name. Percy George became a mechanic and garage owner, the name still lives on in P.G. Forryan Limited in Bell Street. His uncle kept the King William IV in Bell Street, the name of his uncle was, of course, John George. John Forryan farmed at Squires Knob Farm in Newgate End, so we see how the family names were perpetuated.

Les Forryan and his wife, Maggie, when he was a soldier in the Army
Service Corps, 1915.

These were brought up in the old house with their parents. I never knew Mr Forryan senior; I am told he was a kindly man who was loved by all. He was a grazier and butcher and served on the old Wigston U.D.C. for some 30 years from its birth in 1896. He was a member and trustee of Wigston Congregational Chapel. He never shaved in his life because his father spent so much time in the barber's that he, William Goodwin Forryan, vowed never to shave if so much time was wasted doing so.

My Grandma Forryan who lived at the top of Bell Street, was a native of Wytham, Oxfordshire. She was introduced to my Grandfather by his sister who was a much travelled lady. She wrote to my Grandfather saying, "I have found a family with some very nice girls in it, I will introduce you". The courtship took place and as I understand it, if it is true that marriages are made in heaven, theirs was.

Grandma told me how as a girl she went to work at Blenheim Palace, (their family farm was possibly on the Blenheim Estate) and what a cold, draughty and damp place the palace was. She was glad to get back home to the small snug farmhouse.

Arnold Forryan farmed Squires Knob Farm in Newgate End. His house was approached down Newgate End from Moat Street, past Yew Tree House on the right and through a narrow gap in the wall across the front. The house faced east and the portion we walked by was a typical two-up-two-down cottage of a fairish age. The older portion which was between this and Yew Tree House was the most interesting. One entered by continuing round the house walking towards the back, as it were, of Yew Tree House. The doorway was in front of you. There was an external chimney. It was built in the narrow brick of the early 1700s. Straight in front was the kitchen with its tiled and brick floor, straight in front of the other side of the kitchen was a half sunken cellar or dairy. Above the dairy was one bedroom. This part of the house was definitely very old.

The farm ran downhill away from the house and had an assortment of farm buildings. At the bottom of the hill was a brook running from the Horsewell Spring (after which Horsewell Lane is named), down to the River Sense near Crow Mills. There was a bridge across the stream at this point and a small dam over which the water used to flow. Adjacent to the dam was the depression of the ancient Manor House moat, it used to be very obvious before Davenport Road was built over it. This was the old wash pit area, where clothes were washed and most likely sheep were dipped, on separate days, we hope!

Arnold loved fat bacon and always seemed to have some hanging in Newgate End Farmhouse. He always went into the Manager's office at the Bank to conduct his business even for deposits or withdrawals. He persisted in doing his banking as he had from the start. A cigarette and, I believe, a small sherry was expected of the Manager. Cheeky perhaps, but I believe Arnold was upholding the tradition of greater personal service of his early years. All his horses were named "Flower", I don't know why, but he was not unique as many farmers did this. Another habit of farmers was sometimes unkindly, to name an animal they had purchased after its vendor. No doubt this caused anger on occasions. I was annoyed when I heard a boar called "Orson".

Few men stood by their word as Les Forryan did. When the land was being developed all round him, he still had 12 acres left in Aylestone Lane by the railway bridge. Mr Wheatcroft made an offer to purchase this land from him for £12,000, which he said, "I will sell excluding the house". Seven days later the Boston Black Chemical Co. (which is now Bostik) offered him £20,000 for the land. He told them that it was sold, they said, "Well it was only on the market a week ago, you couldn't have sold it". Uncle Les replied, "No, I have given my word". Despite all the entreaties of Boston Black Chemicals for him to sell, where they reminded him that he had signed nothing, so the previous agreement wasn't binding, he said "I don't have to sign, my word is my bond and I have sold the land to Mr Wheatcroft". Mr Wheatcroft I believe sold the land to B.B. Chemicals retaining a portion for his own workshop and offices. I could wish we all were capable of honouring our word as honestly and sincerely as Les Forryan.

VILLAGE CHARACTERS

During my researches for the two volumes of *Bygone Wigston*, I became aware of the closeness of the Wigston Community. Almost everyone seems once to have been related – Old Pegg Kinshin lived at Mowsley End and he took great pride in telling me he was related to me. My mother said, "There are certain relatives that you don't want to remember, even if they are as distant as Pegg". He used to hobble along on his stick, have an allotment up Wharf Road alongside the one my father had, and could drink like a fish!

In addition to relatives and family friends, Wigston had a host of fascinating characters who certainly deserve to be remembered.

Let's start with Gloomy Randle who used to look after the gas collector's two wheeled truck while the gasman was emptying the meters around the village. When the ladies passed by his favourite remark was "Gloomy today Ma'am".

Matt Russell, was a stalwart at the old Congs (the Congregational Church). In the services Matt's voice rang loud and clear above everyone else. His full name was Matthew Molesworthy Russell. I did ask him if there was any connection between his name and the field in Wigston on Newton Lane opposite Ashpole spinney, which was called "Mole pen". Molesworth was a family name however and he doubted if there was a connection. Matt Russell loved his Chapel and when one of the cars at his funeral broke down a delay of 20 minutes occurred before the cortege could move. Relatives were very distressed, but someone remarked "Matt to the last tried to stay with his beloved Church". The world is poorer for the loss of men like Matt Russell, he was a fine Christian gentleman.

In the 1860s a forebear, George Russell, constantly stood for election

Les Forryan and Harold Boulter sowing "Prince of Prussia" peas, 1963.
This variety has been grown in Wigston since the 1860s.

for the Parish Meeting. Each time the words "ineligible for election, no property" appeared. He fought on but no record of his ever being elected appears.

One of the most likeable rogues that I knew was Albert Palfrey. I first came into contact with Albert when I was assisting with the threshing on my uncle Les' farm. At lunch break and dinner times, I would chat with Albert and others.

One day Albert and his family were out driving up Wardley Hill and coming out of a side road they bumped into another car. This really frightened him because his car was not taxed, but Albert had got the gift of the gab and, eventually, the man whose car had been hit whilst innocently travelling on his lawful way gave Albert £5 for damage to Albert's car!

Albert had convinced him that he was speeding down the road and if he had been going at a normal speed he would not have hit Albert. I said, "Albert surely that's not true". He replied, "No, but I wasn't going to have the police along and prosecute me and he seemed so eager to give me some money towards my damage, I should have been a fool to refuse".

The Cong's – Congregational (now United Reformed) Chapel,
Long Street, about 1935.

When I was a paper lad one of the terrors of my life was delivering Albert's paper. He lived then in a little cottage up Spa Lane, which used to belong to the Wyggeston Hospital. Albert had a dog, a Collie, a long-legged one and it was a vicious brute, it would bite anyone on sight. One day in fact Albert could not get into his own house because the dog was in a mood. When I went in my van in latter years to see him, I used to sit in the van and wait at the door until someone came out to lock the dog up. I think there was quite a degree of rejoicing in Spa Lane the day Albert's Collie dog died.

Albert worked for me in his latter years and was always a good employee. He was an old faithful of the Liberal Club and even when he was poorly he would sit there enjoying the life going on around him. If all the old hands of today were as straightforward and as harmless as Albert, the world would be a lot better place.

Another character, or characters, were the Copsons. One Copson worked on the cemetery and used to do the mowing. A very, very ancient man, I knew him for many years and he always looked very old, but what a craftsman with a scythe! He would mow section 'A' which everyone else cursed because of the amount of mounds and edgings. He would mow it beautifully as if it had been trimmed by scissors, never seeming to rush, always honing his scythe razor sharp and working with a beautiful swish action. A Mr Hubbard also mowed the cemetery.

Tut Copson was a small man who always wore a bowler hat, he used to laugh and say "The best thing made, you don't get a wet head with a bowler, the brim shoots it over the back of the shoulder". Old Tut showed me how to tag a sheep. With his hand shears he would clip the mucky wool off the tail, expose the maggots, slide his hand in his old tattered coat pocket and produce a bottle of some mysterious liquid which he would pour on the affected part, "Right lad, that will clear it", he would say, "Let it go", and off would go the sheep happily free of maggots.

One day he was telling me about a hayfork he was using, with his weird chuckle, he said, "Well I might as well use it cos' he don't want it now". I asked him why the owner didn't need it. "Cos' he's been up cemetery the last 10 years and he'd hardly want hayfork would he?" he retorted.

One day up the farm he and Sonny Hurst were attacked by an owl or a kestrel, I remember them bringing the bird into the old farmhouse kitchen in Bell Street and showing it to us. We lads were really in awe of this bird. What prompted the attack I don't know, perhaps they had disturbed its nest. In his latter years Tut went to live in the almshouses. He told me with pride when he had been accepted for residence. "I went to see some gentlemen and they said, 'Do you live in Wigston?' Well," he said, "I had to laugh and I told 'em I were born alongside the Bell Inn, just fancy them not knowing who I was". He got his little cottage in the almshouses and joined the happy band that lived there.

The Davenports, an old Wigston family, were the last people recorded as living in the Old Manor House, which was described by John Nichols, the county's historian, as being in ruins in the late eighteenth century. It was a rubble stone built house. One time it was one of the early meeting places of the independents who later became Congregationalists. The site is commemorated in the name of Davenport Road, which today occupies roughly the same spot. No proper archaeological excavation was done in the area. I did look into the road works carried on at the time and found a considerable number of animal bones possibly from the kitchens of the house. What with the speed of the machinery and complete disinterest by responsible bodies, nothing could be properly investigated.

Aerial view of Ruben Rawlins' farm, Kilby Bridge, 1950s. Very much the same view was seen by the Polish Airforce pilots on training runs during the Second World War.

At the end of the Little Hill Estate near the railway, overlooking Kilby Bridge, still stands a small farm house called Kilby Bridge Lodge. Ruben Rawlins lived there, "Rube Rollins" to the locals. One day during the Second World War Mrs Rawlins was in Leicester when some Polish airmen came up to her and said, "Ah! you are the lady by the railway". She was surprised at this until they informed her that this stretch of line was used by them in their Wellington bombers as a training run. The Polish crews had flown over so often and taken so many photos of this area that they recognised Mrs Rawlins.

Rawlins were pig farmers and at one time there were four large farms in Wigston with a population of some 6,000 pigs; a lot of pork and bacon. Most allotments in Magna and South had numerous pig sties and pigs. Wigston was at that time also self-supporting in milk.

My neighbour on the allotments was a very kind gentleman by the name of Ernie Wooley, who lived in Moat Street opposite Crease's the old butcher's shop. He was the grave digger at Wigston. Ernie always had an open necked shirt, no matter how cold it was, at which I used to marvel. He had pride in his cemetery and he kept it in apple pie order. We used

A glass-sided hearse in a funeral procession along Station Road, 1920s

to go in the summer and buy the hay from the men who mowed the cemetery and cart it away on the horse and dray. Woe betide us if we cut the corners and the iron wheels damaged the edges of the grass. Sometimes if we left the dray in an inconvenient place, Ernie and his colleague, Freddie Edwards, would push it back into position elsewhere! The hay used to be cobbed and was full of herbs so the cattle ate it readily.

With the sombre talk of burials I am reminded of an old lady who lived in North Street, Mrs Sharpe. She had a very large nose, which fascinated us children, with one or several warts upon it. She intrigued us because she was the lady who "laid them out". When anyone died Mrs Sharpe was fetched and we were told "She stretched them on a board so they went stiff straight".

When we were loading hay on another occasion, I said to my Uncle Les Forryan, "Who is John Forryan?"

"Uncle John, where's he?", he asked. "You're standing on him!" I replied. Uncle John, I believe, is recorded in White's *Directory* as a victualler – a publican, and kept the King William IV. Nearby was Abraham Forryan and he used to farm at Squires Knob Farm and was a type of Parish Councillor in 1850.

"Old" Moore was a roadman and a very stout gentleman indeed. He kept the roads neat and tidy. A day or two after he died, Uncle Les and I were in the cemetery and Ernie Wooley was preparing his grave. We said we hoped he'd got the measurements right!

He said "No need to measure!"

The following day when we saw Ernie we asked, "How did it go?"

"Perfect" he replied, "It fitted him like a glove!"

Old Moore lived in a thatched cottage in Bull Head Street. He was responsible for the cleanliness of the A.50 from the Leicester boundary in Wigston Fields to the Kilby boundary just past the "Stanbrig" or Sence Bridge and every grip was kept clean and tidy. Regrettably Ernie Wooley died prematurely of a heart attack, even the toughest of us have to succumb in due course. I shall remember him for the great deal of advice on pig-keeping which he gave me in my early days.

Shipps the coal merchants had a tall horse which hauled their cart. One day the pole which was used to prop up the shafts when the cart stood empty, fell down and Arthur Marlow, one of the coalmen who was high up in the cart, asked me (a very nervous small boy), to clip the pole up – "Boy was I frit !"

Here is a portion of a Miss Shipp's diary of 1879, a graphic tale of the times! This is a memorandum for the year, but every day she kept a diary, weather, gossip, news, temperatures:

Winter of 1878–79 very severe. Frost from December 1st for eleven weeks.

Snow fell October 31st, 1878. No Spring weather, very cold in June and July, never did without a fire. Went to Hastings in July for a month. E.M. came for a few days. Had a bad attack of haemorrhage August 7th. Father and Grandpa came. Eddie went home. Mr & Mrs & Miss M. came for the day. Never too warm to do without an overcoat. Saw Dr. Johnson 3 times. Ret'n home August 25th very wet and dull. Was able to get out at times until the Friday in the feast week. Had a good seed time; no rain for several weeks in October. Wheat was carried at Newton on the 12th October. Very severe weather set in early. Sunday December 7th the coldest day. Registered 25 deg. of frost or 7 degrees fah. in the garden at 9 a.m. My room never reached 50 deg. with a good fire all day. A great deal of skating. I was 21 years old on December 12th. Had a great many presents - all of them much prized as gifts as well from their being valuable. Mamma very unwell during the Spring. Baby born April 5th. Mamma had a very bad leg afterwards. Grandma very ill. Did not see her after 15th March. Lizzie Cuthbert away staying with Emma for six weeks. Emma Cuthbert died March 13th. Grandma died May 28th.

Joe Wignall was quite a writer of letters to the press etc. He made a bet in the pubs that he would have kidney beans in flower in winter, March at the latest. Quite a considerable "book" was taken. Joe turned up with his beans, they were kidney beans right enough, that no one could deny, they were in "flower", some of the nicest plain flour anyone could wish to see!

Whether he got thumped for this joke I don't know.

My grandfather's waggoner was named Mason who reared 13 children and said it was always his ambition to have a baker's dozen. This probably explains the numbers of Masons in Wigston. Mr Mason came up one day whilst we were milking and said he was really disgusted because someone had levelled out the "rig and thurror" in the old foot road field. "What's the town coming to", he asked. The foot road is now the extra annexe to the Willow Park. There was quite a large pond there which caused considerable problems when the Council built their houses along the front of Aylestone Lane. I well remember old waggoner Mason telling me of working a mare in foal (this was an accepted practice providing you didn't back her). This particular mare foaled actually whilst she was in the shafts. A horse foaling is rather violent and it must have caused quite a bit of panic.

He also told of the well in Aylestone Lane which he claimed was deeper than the railway cutting. One day a man went down the well to examine it. To do this they lowered a ladder down the well, put a crowbar through the ladder near the top to support it. When the ladder was in place he started to climb down. "I'll just test it", he said and gave a jump. He was a very heavy man and the rungs of the ladder started to snap through and down he went. The bottom rung had a wire support through it and this held him. A very frightened and quietened man was rescued from the well, considerably bruised in both body and spirit.

A character of old Wigston was Harry Bartram; he wasn't really from Wigston, he came from "Chinatown", over the bridge along Aylestone Lane. When the estate was built, the houses were occupied before electricity arrived. So many candles and lamps were used that it seemed like the English image of China. He was a really gypsy type, he wore a neckachief. He had a little pony, when he dressed it up to go out it even had ear caps with little bells. A fascinating sight was old Harry dressed up with his pony to match. Whilst on holiday in Ross-on-Wye, I saw a horse and cart being used for the carting of street refuse, the horse had on ear muffs similar to Harry's pony, I asked the driver why these were worn. He told me they were to stop the flies and midges getting into the ears. This was a common practice when working in the woods.

Waterleys' playground now stands on part of Harry's old allotment.

George Willett was another well known Wigston name. He farmed "on the bank" and his house was pulled down (to my mind thoughtlessly) to make way for a sewer. Part of his land is now the access path through to Boulter Crescent. George is immortalized on one of Donald Green's prints of old Wigston. He was the last man to work a horse and cart in Wigston and in the winter he had his horse well wrapped up with old coats. George was a benefactor in a way, he would go around any waste bit of ground, scythe the grass off and bring it down in his horse and cart for his cattle. If the weather was bad, or if the horse was off colour, he would push the grass in a wheelbarrow. George was a very old fashioned farmer, but what a wonderful man to talk to, his knowledge was really fantastic, I wonder what formal education he received? I have some old swingle trees dated at least 200 years old, which I got from George's yard when the buildings were pulled down. Also a cheese press and a fireplace which are now in my Wigston Museum.

Kilby Bridge was the home of another old character of the district, a Mr Hastletine, an elderly gentleman who in the '30s lived in one of a pair of thatched cottages on the left far side of the present Kilby Bridge leaving Wigston. Mr Hastletine had a beard and was always in an embroidered smock. He was very fond of wearing a sack as an apron. There was no water in these two cottages, so he fetched his water in two buckets on a yoke from the communal tap in Ellis yard, which was at the side of the Navigation Inn. Children were very fond of him, when they visited him he would make a little cornet-shaped cup out of newspaper, put in two teaspoonsful of sugar and they would gaily dip their fingers in and suck it off -they had their own 'dab and sucker'.

The Pochin family of Wigston owned land all over the place. They were one of the instigators of the 'Enclosure Act', which caused a lot of ill feeling here as elsewhere in England. The land was enclosed by Act of Parliament, Surveyors came from London and planned it out. They did an exceedingly good job. The hedges followed the natural drainage and contours and the shapes of most of the fields were very logical. Many were small because each person who owned land before the enclosures had some allocated to him. However, there was a time limit for digging and planting boundary ditches and hedges and these poor peasants just hadn't the money to do it. They also had to contribute to enclose the Lord of the Manor's land free of charge. Many therefore, had to sell their land. However, the Pochins retained some of their lands, and one lot was up Newton Lane where a farmhouse called "Alfrace" now stands.

My grandfather, William Goodwin Forryan, was tenant of this particular field for many years. When the field was sold, my grandfather was most upset that he as tenant, hadn't been given the opportunity to purchase it and knew nothing of the deal until it was completed. He told Mr Pochin that this was "not the act of a gentleman". Mr Pochin was so upset to think a man could say he wasn't a gentleman, he threatened to withhold his gift to the Parish of the clock in the church tower. Now no one seems to give a damn whether they are gentlemen or not.

In front of the United Reform Church in Long Street, there is a tomb to one of the Pochin's family, erected I think some 40 or 50 years after this man's death. He must have been quite revered and quite a man to

Glen Parva Barracks, about 1920. Here Major Stoney Smith is presenting
long service medals to the troops.

have a memorial placed there so many years after his death. There is a
record in the chapel minute book dated October 12th, 1915. Mr W
Pochin asked permission of the Trustees to raise and improve the
monument over his late father's grave, so it does seem that there is a
grave under his monument. It was proposed that Mr Pochin be asked to
raise the whole front of the Chapel Yard at the same time, also he was
asked to invest enough money, the interest of which to be used for
keeping the monument in repair. On 1 May 1917 the Secretary reported
that Mr W Pochin had refused to invest the money to carry out the work
on the monument, so the try-on fell through.

About that time the old tales of Orson Wright were floating around
and here again I am indebted to Uncle Les for telling me when Orson
Wright built South Wigston he intended it to be a twin city alongside
Leicester. He planned a complete environment and whatever criticism
may be made of him, in his day, he did a thorough job providing homes,
factories, hotels, the Church, everything, a complete town. He put green
play areas at the ends of many of the streets, which the wise men
following decided were not needed as such and were built on. Now the

Blaby Road, South Wigston

Blaby Road, South Wigston, looking west, 1920s. On the right is Orson Wright's house.

need shouts at us, yet we build on the school playing fields. But nevertheless Orson Wright said that one thing stopped him in his tracks. He negotiated with the Wheatsheaf Works (the Co-op) to build their Shoe Factory at South Wigston. He thought he had the whiphand and hung on for his price. The Co-op changed their idea and built their factory at Clarendon Park. This really halted the development of South Wigston.

Bill Gunning the old Council Clerk used to tell with a chuckle of when an election was held and Orson Wright being carried on the shoulders of a cheering crowd calling out, "Orson Wright champion of the working man".

"Monkey" Lee would stride through the village from Two Steeples factory and along Central Avenue, to see Miss Eddie King. He was always a gay (in the traditional sense), almost gaudily dressed man in the height of fashion. The smell of perfume flooded the avenue as Eddie bathed, and the locals gossiped. His nickname came because his father once called him a "Young Monkey".

There was Oliver Sibson with his deformed leg who kept the outdoor beer licence. Cruelly, we used to call him "half man, half girder", because he had quite a considerable bit of ironwork on his leg, but he could make quite a considerable speed, although the bad leg was almost doubled up under the knee.

"Dissa" Boulter was a window cleaner who lost a hand in the First World War, but he could certainly whip round and get the windows of the village done. One other memorable occasion was a party and presentation to the late William Boulter V.C. A platform was erected on "The Bank" beside the Queen Victoria Jubilee Fountain to welcome him back home after winning his award in France. He also gave a talk in the Long Street Board School where he was educated. The Council and local big-wigs comprised the platform party and an address was given by the Council Chairman.

"Chirper" Vann got his nickname for his bird connections. He bred and kept canaries, he caught bull finches and linnets. He also had a lot of "milky does"!

Let's explain. In the spring rabbitting in large numbers means catching does which are feeding young. So, some people will only have buck rabbits, but if skinned and dressed who knows the difference?

However, Chirper told a lady who wanted only a buck rabbit, because the rabbits were breeding – "Lady, I have knowledge and purchase from a farmer who keeps his does in one field and bucks in another, he only mixes them in the Spring". "Oh! how thoughtful", replied the lady, "I'll have some of the buck rabbits"!

Billy, alias Tiny Clarke sold fresh mackerel and poultry from a basket which he plucked in his scruffy house near the 'Horse and Trumpet'. He bedded the feathers into the floor of the house inches thick. The whole place stank but Tiny plied his trade and spent his money in the pub. He eventually moved to a shop at the corner of Bell Street.

"Alka" Robinson lived in Bull Head Street. His father was a cobbler who used to make hand made shoes in Spa Lane. He had individual lasts for clients with bits of leather tacked on where bunions and corns had deformed their feet. Alka was the man who introduced me to paraffin in the war and showed me how to perfect the mixture of petrol and paraffin, to eke out the petrol rations we had – "Don't put too much paraffin in lad or otherwise the engine will glow". He also showed me how to put red petrol through a gasmask filter to get most of the dye out, so that it could enhance the petrol ration!

One of the Edwards family, a brother of Freddie Edwards, who was a colleague of Ernie Wooley the grave digger, used to work for Mr Pask

Wigston's First World War hero, Sergeant W E Boulter, VC, and a Miss
F Lusher, about 1918.

who was one of the local farmers producing milk. A lad I worked with later on by the name of Alan Towers (nicknamed "Wimpy") recounted how he took delight when milking, in squibbing Edwards on the back. Edwards didn't react, he carried on with his milking until he had finished. Quite carefully and slowly he put down his milking stool, turned round to Wimpy with the full bucket of milk in his hand and tipped it right over his head leaving him sitting there saturated with an upturned bucket on his head. It was instant justice. He didn't report what Roger Pask's reaction was to losing his milk. Fred's brother, "Friday" Edwards, worked for farmer "Quizy" Hurst at Newton Harcourt – nicknames again.

George Russell who lived in Cedar Avenue, a character who had a fantastic memory of old Wigston, told me there was at one time a jail house at the top of Spa Lane. His favourite tale was of the Putchin family. One day in the middle of the sermon in All Saint's Church, one of Mr Putchin's workmen walked down the aisle and attempted to whisper in his ear. Mr Putchin was quite annoyed at someone interrupting his doze, or rapt attention of the sermon and said "Speak up louder man, what do you want"? The rather nervous labourer said "I want me money Mr Putchin". It was the habit in those days to pay the men on Sunday, as the butchers' shops and grocers' did not close until midday. This man was most insistent that his wages be paid because the butcher's shop would soon be shut and his family would have no meat for their Sunday dinner. After Mr Putchin's insistence to speak up, he shouted out "Give me my money I've got to get some meat for Sunday dinner".

"Poppy" Abbot was another who lived in Bell Street in the house now Dalbys. He was a member of the Carl Rosa Opera Company and took the tenor solos for a number of years. During the summer he could be seen and heard practising his scales on the piano with his windows open. At that time I was working opposite to his window and we would annoy him by whistling and he would come to the window and swear or made rude gestures. He lived with his widowed mother and a man servant. The mother was housebound and was taken for walks daily in a bath chair. One day Poppy took her up the Aylestone Lane and left her after she refused him money for a drink (at that time he was drinking heavily).

Jimmy Moore was the celebrated village hedge cutter and was paid 8d a chain for his splendid workmanship. It was a treat to get him in Sam Laundon's saddlers shop where the local farmers gathered to collect their repaired harness. The favourite talk was the weather and Jimmy said he could forecast by studying the stars. A lot of leg pulling was done in that shop.

Many will remember Squib Allsop's barbers shop on Leicester Road close to Peabody's (now Wilkinson's) watch repair shop. This was a hive of gossip and local scandals. It was taken on later by his son Stan.

A favourite with the ladies at that time was "Long Fan" who lived in a house (now pulled down) opposite the laundry. She was the village fortune teller and lived with Tommy Bowley who was a blacksmith's striker at Tom Smith's forge, now Adcock's petrol station. It was during the war years she did a brisk business with people asking for help on missing persons and prisoners of war.

Another well known character in the Little Hill area was Tommy Cross, otherwise known as "Juicy". He had no regular employment, haymaking and harvesting were his main source of employment and a little cattle droving to Leicester Cattle Market. He filled his time up by opening the gate into Wistow Park for the traffic of that time and was usually rewarded by a copper. The nickname arose from the gurgle of his clay pipe which carried more juice than tobacco.

BAR ROOM CHARACTERS

Who was the barber who lived opposite the 'Horse and Trumpet'?

Half way through cutting the hair he would ask the customer for payment. He would take the money and go across to the 'Horse and Trumpet' leaving the victim sitting there with his hair half cut, unable to go home until the money was spent and the job completed.

And who was the unnamed gentleman who fell out bitterly with the old Cong's chapel authorities, vowing he would never again enter the chapel precincts?

One day he left his horse tied up outside the 'Shoulder of Mutton' in Long Street. When he returned he discovered to his horror that his horse had been stolen. Before he could contact the police, however, he discovered where it was!

Some wags had taken it to the chapel yard and tethered it there. No one would unhitch his horse and he had to enter the yard to get his horse back.

There was a man in Wigston prosecuted by the police for being drunk in charge of a horse and cart. The horse and cart was coming along Long Street, the man lay in the back of the cart, incapable, the horse obviously knew his way home.

One hedge-cutting yarn was of a man in a pub one wet day. He had obviously had one or two and an argument started about who had got the sharpest billhook. Without hesitation, he whipped out his billhook and chopped off the table leg with one clean sweep. The landlord was not amused.

One is lost now, the old familiar landmarks have gone. The Jubilee Fountain on the "Bank" and the old public houses such as the 'King William' in Bell Street, the 'Bull's Head' and 'Travellers Rest' in Bull Head Street and not forgetting the 'Durham Ox' in Long Street and also the long row of Almshouses on the opposite side of the lane. Ben Hackett was known as mine host of the 'Crown' and also Higwell known as Ernest who at one time kept the 'Horse and Trumpet'. It's many years since the "United" played in the field behind the 'Trumpet' which boasted some well known and talented players.

When the 'Travellers Rest' was discontinued Mr A H Broughton worked it as a hosiery factory and by degrees pulled it down and rebuilt it to its present state. The pub was run by Mr Boothaway and there was a weekly sight of Joey Gee lowering the barrels of beer into the cellar after being carted from the goods yard in South Wigston. One of Mr Boothaway's daughters married Charlie Lewin's son, Charlie who owned and ran the factory in Mowsley End, the factory made material on the old hand frames and worked by treadle power.

At the rear of the pub a row of thatched cottages filled the remainder of the area and were pulled down around 1910. It was known as "Flea Alley", one house opposite the farm gates had at one time been the village gaol. The farm was run by Mr Albert Shipp, a well known farmer and sportsman.

I often heard Levi Sampson refer to "Mother Minty", who kept a pub at Kilby. Her lavatory had two seats side by side. It must have been amusing sitting side by side and having a chat! Some of the old hands still refer to the double-one at darts as a "Mother Minty".

Ken Roe recalled for me that his grandfather told him of Irish labourers who came into Wigston at seasonal times mainly to cut the corn with sickles, this they did on piece work. They would go into either the 'Bull's Head' or the 'Travellers Rest' and buy a tot of whisky. Whisky would be poured onto the table and a match put to it. If it burned they would stay and drink there, if not, they would curse the landlord for being a rogue and watering his whisky, then leave. Even without the mass of legislation we have, labourers did devise ways to look after themselves.

Chapter Three
Childhood and Growing Up

My memories of childhood revolve around two places, home (especially the kitchen and its food) and the streets of Wigston, where much of my time was spent from an early age.

HOME LIFE

As I mentioned before, I was born in a terraced house in Bell Street, the fourth child in a family of eight. Just before it was demolished I entered it, looked around at the rooms and thought, good heavens however did we all get in? The front room was a drapers shop and the rear room a small kitchen. There was an even smaller pantry beyond. Upstairs were two bedrooms with an attic over the top. The toilet was up the yard next to the coal shed, near the pump. The long garden was shared with two other houses, a joint entry for the three houses. This was the scene of my childhood.

Mother ran the shop and the home, father hawked his drapery around the villages in his little van, so we children certainly had to muck in but we had lots of time to play. On occasion, father would put a plate of food in the centre of the table, he would then wind up the gramophone, we would walk round the table, when the music stopped we would all dive in. All of us were fast eaters.

We were very poor in those days, but we were always clean and mother and father were proud that we were so. We often had to scratch around to get money to nip across to Billy Cox's shop for milk. It was a fantastic special treat when we had jelly for Sunday tea. During the week it was bread, butter and home-made jam if we were lucky. There was a dessert called "hay making pudding"; what we didn't finish at dinner we put jam on and ate at tea-time when it was re-christened "cake"!

On one occasion when we had company, the table was opened to have an extra leaf put in and a pile of crusts dropped on to the floor. The reason for this was the time-honoured "You can have your jelly if you eat up your bread and butter first" approach!

We just ate the centre and tucked the crusts under the ledge of the table!

When there was a flood or heavy rain, we could not go into the pantry. The well was beneath and the floor would flood to a depth of between 12 to 18 inches. We always had beautiful tea because the water was drawn from this well. The kettle used to get a lime coating though; it was said that Wigston folks had tough bones because of the amount of lime in the water we drank.

Cleaning the house was always a large chore for my Aunt Jessie. Immediately after the kitchen floor had been washed, newspapers were laid to protect the clean floor. It was not very often that the floor saw light of day. Tea leaves were sprinkled on the carpets (damp leaves preferred) and then the carpet was brushed. This simple expediency kept down the dust, although Uncle Les did have a hand operated vacuum cleaner which damn near killed anyone pumping it to create the vacuum. He also had his own electricity up at Goldhill Stores produced by a little petrol engine which went putt, putt, putt, like a little machine gun, the exhaust sticking out a hole in the wall. The electricity it produced was stored in rows and rows of glass tanks with cells like large car batteries. The house and the farm buildings were lit by this, not a very good light but far better than by hurricane lanterns.

At Christmas time the whole of the family went to Grandma Forryan's. Ernie the butcher provided the turkey, Cecil the chemist put on the film show at night, -silent films with Charlie Chaplin and Felix the Cat. I can vividly remember the camel in one of the Felix films drinking the Nile dry and its hump swelling and swelling, the camel and Felix walking across the dry Nile, and the camel spitting water back into the Nile and the hump subsiding. My cousin still has the camera and films but what masterpieces those films were to us children. Rubber gloves were worn to operate the camera which was also stood on a pile of newspaper, so obviously it was a live frame!

It was grand when someone came to play the piano and we all had a good old sing-song. Then father came forth with his singing, and mother would rebuke him saying that he had learned so many of these songs in the pubs. But they were not vulgar, and father never never did sing all the songs *I* knew, these I learnt at the Scouts and other such organisations!

Over Christmas we waited excitedly for the "Congs" choir to come and sing the carols. One Christmas they towed an organ around Wigston on a sledge to accompany their singing. There was a very "strong" choir. It was early hours of Christmas morning before they got home, tired, but I am sure happy after their singing. The following are two of the carols we children sang:-

1.
I 'ave a little whistle bob made out of 'olly tree
The finest little whistle bob that ever you did see
For it is a Christmas tune an' we travel far an' near
An' we wish yer good 'ealth an' a Happy Noo Year.

Good Mistress an' good master if yer both do be in
I've a little pocket to put my money in
For it is a Christmas tune an' we travel far an' near
An' we wish yer good 'ealth an' a Happy Noo Year.

2.
Christmas is a coming, the geese are getting fat,
Please put a penny in the old man's hat,
If yer 'aven't gort a penny a ha'peney will do,
If yer 'aven't gort a ha'peney God Bless you.

When we went out carol singing, two three or even more of us, we often sang "I had a little whistle bob". I was unaware that this version of the carol was PURE Leicestershire.

EARNING MY KEEP

As children, we were all expected to do work around the house or run errands. In this way we not only helped out, but also earned a little pocket money.

One of our chores was to take bucket and shovel to collect droppings from horses for the garden. Storeys the bakers horse drawn van was a damned nuisance, their long stop outside our house inevitably meant a shout "Duncan go and get the hoss muck". Every Saturday afternoon, we would trek to the large allotments in Newton Lane, Welford Road and Horsewell Lane, stopping on the way to collect the horse droppings as we passed along the road.

We as children would fetch coke for anyone for a few coppers. We also fetched creosote and the tar to paint fowl pens and fences, and we usually got ourselves well gummed up in the process. To see the coke produced at the gasworks was quite a fascinating thing for us; water was poured on hot coals and great clouds of steam rose. We used to fetch coke for various people in a wheelbarrow. A close friend of mine, a lad by the name of Jack Bradshaw, used to go with his barrow and fetch the coke up for the Burdett's in Ball Dyke for their ovens for cooking meat and pies.

Children used to collect "hose" for toeing and they tried to get light coloured ones if their mothers' eyes were poor. The boys also had to "unrove" the socks or prepare them for toeing and iron them before linking. The socks were called Griswalds, after the machinery for making them.

Bell Street School, 1930s. The bell is now on display in my museum.

The chemist would refill your smelling salts bottle for sixpence. One day, when my father was a boy, he had been to get a bottle refilled and the village bully took the bottle from my father. Not believing it was smelling salts, he took a deep sniff, nearly suffocated and slung the bottle away in temper, then hit father, who got another clip when he got home for losing the bottle.

I believe it was Burton Overy where children went with the threshing gangs and caught mice, put them in paper bags and took them to school. They released them, much to the annoyance and anger of the teacher and it was said the school suffered from mice for many a year afterwards.

STREET LIFE

When not at school or doing work around the house, we spent most of our time out of doors, running errands or just playing in the street with other children.

At the top of Bell Street, lived Dr Briggs, in what was then a grand house. He was blind, and when he came along the street (invariably

A classroom and pupils of Bell Street School, about 1931. In the right hand corner of the room was the school bell rope and it was a special honour for pupils to be allowed to pull this.

dressed in plus-fours) tapping away with his white stick, we children would make certain that he knew we were there, not to trip him up. So we chatted away as loudly as we could and he would say, "Hello children, how many are there of you?", we would tell him the number and he would then open a little box like a snuff box, fetch out some dolly mixtures and give us one each. Woe betide us if we said there were more than there actually was, because he could count the voices!

One day I was very clever and daring! Ernie Bradshaw was going up Bell Street with the horse and dray, I tied my trolley on the back and bowled along in style, cheering and laughing at everyone. This was all very good until we started to go downhill. The horse sat in the breeching, (that is it leaned back into its harness) and with my momentum I overtook the dray and underneath I went. Ernie was a rotten devil, he just laughed, but Grandma made a beautiful job of patching me up. Granny Forryan patched me up many a time after I had come adrift from my trolley, and I think I have left more than my fair share of flesh on Newton Lane Hill, Bell Jetty corner etc. Grandma being such a gentle old lady she would not hurt me by using iodine and such horrible weapons that mother used.

Young and old used to swim in the canal. Double rail lock was a favourite bathing place. We also used to go down to the old baths at South Wigston. They were by the canal locks at the back of the High School, and were surrounded by corrugated iron fencing, the top of which had been cut to form a saw tooth top to discourage unofficial attendance! These baths were the only swimming facility Wigston had for years and canal water was used. When certain attendants swept the surround they swept the refuse into the baths, unhygienic all the way round! When I became a councillor, I had a good opportunity to fight and obtain proper swimming baths for Wigston.

A wonderful benefactor to Oadby, Mrs Ellis, donated a swimming pool to Oadby, and Wigston lads used to go there, that is if the Oadby lads didn't catch them going and give them a good hiding for being so cheeky as to enter Oadby.

We used to love to stand on the footbridge on the south side of the level crossing and cough and gasp in the smoke as the trains went beneath. It was ironic that when British Rail decided they wanted to bring their electrified line from Rugby to Leicester, they found that they had already sold a portion of the land to Atkinson's. The death of the railway line was sealed for all time.

A lot of the games we played in the streets were seasonal. "Whip and top" was the favourite one which seemed always to come out on Shrove Tuesday. The whip was a simple stick with a leather boot-lace or a bit of string tied to it. The top was either shaped like a wide cone nearly always with a metal point, or like a 'T'. The whiplash was wrapped round the top, and you would then spin the top off and keep whipping it down the road.

Another seasonal game was with the old chestnuts or "conkers". At Easter you could go to Hallaton to watch or take part in the "bottle kicking", but then you would have to bike it. Biking was more a pastime and the old hands I am told used to have cycling clubs – this was about the turn of the century and these would go off with their old bone-shakers, horrible looking bikes, but to them beautiful. People could travel at virtually no cost, just under their own leg power.

"Snobs" was a favourite all the year round.

These were an assortment of shapes, usually four cubes with a round ball. You would hold them in the palm of your hand, throw them in the air and then try to catch at least one on the back of your hand. On the next throw you would have to catch two, and then one more each successive throw. Then a sequence would be set up whereby you would pick one up between two fingers and do the throwing up in the air and catching on the back of the hand process, again holding increasing numbers of snobs between the fingers. The most difficult move being to lodge the round ball on the hand.

"Fag cards" was another game. Here a cigarette card was stood against the wall and one skimmed the others and knocked it down. Collecting cigarette cards was quite a craze as well as stamp collecting. Cards were obviously popular, especially by small boys, who played pontoon. Lads I knew used to play at cards in a little pigeon hut. They would also nip over the orchard to Mrs Pimms on Ball Dyke, where the winner could buy some of the goodies that she used to sell in her general store with the farthings and halfpennies he had won.

A playground game was "Jonny Mopp", where a boy would stand against the wall as a type of cushion. The boys would split into two teams and between two and five boys would bend down, one with his head against the boy by the wall. The idea was for the other boys to come along, leap frog onto them, rest on their backs, until all the boys were on. If the cushion team collapsed they had to give those leapfrogging another go. If the cushion team held for the count of ten, then they changed places. There was a further complication to the rules, where there were three positions for the cushion team, one very low (where the boys were crouching), another half crouching and a third virtually standing, so you had to leapfrog at quite a considerable height.

A night game was "Trollup", which was a weird sort of game. We ran round the streets at night, preferably when it was dark chasing someone and making a general noise and being a nuisance! We youngsters used to think it was the height of growing up if allowed by the bigger ones to play Trollup.

One of my favourites was what we called a "wide game" in the scouts. You would have to, by varying means, penetrate a cordon of scouts across any area of fields. I was a very nervous individual and possibly because of my nervousness, I would manage to wiggle myself on my stomach along some hedge bottom and hide in a tree until they had gone by, or rather cheekily out flank them.

A good old game was playing with the brook, Blackwell Dyke (this is the oldest dyke name in Wigston and it runs from Newton Lane through to Welford Road). A simple earth dam could soon be constructed and the water channelled into varying directions. Boats could be made quite easily and sailed down this little stream, the boat only had to be a twig and imagination did the rest. If anyone turned up from the farming fraternity and if we had our wits about us and kept a look out, we would dodge them and probably yell some cheeky remark as we ran. If we weren't we had the clip of the ear, accept it as such and didn't dare go home and tell our parents.

Uncle Les told me that when he was a boy one of their sports was to stand in an entry, wait until a horse came trotting by, then roll a stone to see if you could hit the horses legs. I can imagine what words came from the waggoners when their horse was subjected to this cruel fun – if the children were caught they got a good thumping.

Swinging on a rope on the branch of a tree was almost seventh heaven, especially as a very brave boy had been up that tree and tied the rope. With ropes, I must not forget the skipping, the old eternal game with its variations and its rhymes, such as "Green gravel, the grass is so green, the fairest young lady that ever was seen".

One of the most daring exploits of all was going up to Rally bridge and putting pennies or halfpennies on the railway line, waiting for the train to go past and see who got the biggest flattened penny. This was not done too often because even the halfpenny could buy two farthing "japs", which were considerable lumps of sweet to chew. Another feat of daring I am told of cyclists was to ride across Blaby Ford, much shallower than it is now. Nevertheless the slightest obstacle in the water would fetch a brave peddler off, much to the joy of his colleagues.

Besides the regular fairs and wakes we were visited by "Holloway's Blood Tub". This was the nickname for a show which was performed on Bassett Street Green, South Wigston. Holloways wintered there with their coke stoves in the Marquee and put on plays such as 'Crippin', 'Maria Martin', 'Sweeney Tod', 'The man they could not hang', and many others. The admission charge was tuppence a time during the First World War.

Sewing was for girls and so was knitting. It was cissy for men to tackle embroidery and crocheting. Boys and men did metal work and wood work. It was a sin to go to the pictures more than once in one week - what extravagance and it was not good for us! It was also not good for us to put salt on tomatoes as it would spoil the flavour (but we did). Vinegar was for fish and chips, not for salads, although salads were only available when we grew our own. It was surprising how much we did grow, we produced our own lettuce till the end of the year. Eggs likewise were a scarcity, as electric light was not yet used to stimulate hens into producing eggs all the year round.

RATTING

Ratting, coursing hares, and shooting were popular as I became older, I even tried fishing once. I did my first shooting with a 28 bore shotgun. A hare popped out of the corn, I was very close and blew its head off. Its ears were still connected by a little bit of skin. Arthur Minney who lived up Aylestone Lane picked it up and said, "Duncan, you've killed it".

A good ratting yarn was told to me by George Gibbons of an old Wigston family. His father was well known for his draining prowess. George told me that when he was a lad whilst threshing, a rat had run up inside the trouser leg of one of the farm hands. The man didn't panic as you or I might have done, but took hold of the bottom of his trouser leg round his knee and hobbled over towards the dog intending to drop the rat for the dog to kill. A boy attempted to hit the rat with a thatch peg. He struck a blow so sharp that he broke the man's leg.

A more amusing tale was of a party of men who were ratting with ferrets. If bitten by a ferret the most immediate first aid was the crude old farm method of "peeing on the wound". If a ferret got hold of anything and would not let go, you used to blow in its face and the ferret would let go. It appears a young lad's ferret had got bitten by a rat. On

"The Bank", at the end of Bell Street, looking east, about 1904. The fountain by the tree was built in 1897 to celebrate the Diamond Jubilee of Queen Victoria's reign. All this was cleared in about 1938 to make way for more traffic. Note the thatched roofs and the sign advertising the market.

the advice of his companions he started to perform the traditional cure, but he omitted to keep his distance. The ferret disliking what was happening, took a bite and the poor lad was in agony. The more he appealed to his colleagues to blow in the ferret's face and make it release him, the more they howled with laughter and rolled around the floor. What happened to this poor fellow's later love life I don't know, but if any of you happen to go ferreting, please remember this lesson.

Modern poisons take care of rats very well, but in doing so remove the necessity of some of the old and, dare one admit, enjoyable country sports. When I was working at the Goldhill Stores Farm and Uncle Les discovered rats in the stable, we would stuff up the holes with sacks and stir the rats out. Uncle Les really was a different character when he had a rat at hand. I tried this dodge much later when a fowl place of mine was heavily infested. I stuffed up the bolt holes, went in, switched on the light. Rats flew in all directions!

One went across my shoulders, that was enough for me, I dived out of that door and settled for subtle poisoning!

Talking of rats there was in the Highcross area of Leicester a rat pit. Women took rats along to the rat pit and sold them for training dogs as ratters. People would bet on their dogs killing the greatest number of rats. These good ladies carried the rats inside their blouses!

If a rat is not trapped, and in the dark, it will not bite. It must have been a spine-chilling sight to see the animated blouses bulging and bobbing with the movement of rats.

CHAPEL HIGH-DAYS AND HOLIDAYS

Summertime "Sermons" and Christmas were the two events when we had new clothes. The Sermons were quite a thing in Wigston. Each church and chapel had these events -Sunday School Anniversaries to give them

A garden tea organised by All Saints' Church, about about 1912. On the left, in a Panama, is Mr Cook, and to the right is Millie Adams. In front of her is Don Ross, in a sailor suit (husband of Gertie Guitina of Nellie Dean fame), and to the right, in a boater, is Harry Harrison. Beyond the tea urn is my grand mother, who is chatting to Miss Hobley. On the extreme right is my aunt Kath.

their full title. A Gallery was put up at the Cong's and the boys sat on the right hand side and the girls on the left. There was a little pulpit arrangement in the middle where the selected best singers would sit. The primary department always sat at the bottom. In its heyday the gallery at Cong's Sermons was full and overflowed into the overhead gallery on each side. I well remember at one Sermon having a pair of shoes which were not quite new, but hellish tight. I took them off, but dropped them and they made a heck of a noise when they fell. I had to wait until the end of the service to duck through the slats of the gallery and recover my shoes. Mr John Stanley has collected the Cong's Chapel Sermons and hymn sheets dating back for some considerable time.

The Harvest Festival was another great occasion. The whole of the front of the Church would be quite liberally covered with fruit, vegetables and flowers. We had an egg, fruit and flower service and a Dr Barnardo's service when we took gifts for the Barnardo's Homes. When the Chapel was decorated, wonderful scroll work was covered on the wall which said, "Peace be within thy walls and prosperity within thy palaces". Mr Hassell was the conductor with a large choir and he would wave his baton and we wondered how on earth people could look at their hymn or anthem books and look at the conductor as well, and thought him quite superfluous and just there to amuse the congregation. The mood has changed now, the Chapel has its active youth organisation, but so many of our traditions have vanished, I believe, forever.

A WARTIME CHILDHOOD

The Second World War obviously had a major impact on life, as it formed the environment in which I left school and started work on the land.

In Cong's chapel yard trenches were dug by the soldiers who were billeted there and many bones were dug up. As children we were intrigued to dig around and find bits of bone left by the soldiers.

One Bank Holiday, the scouts were going on a trek, not with the trek carts, but merely with our ruck sacks on, billy-cans at the ready to go off, when a plane came over and one lad said, "look it's a Hampden", which was a British bomber. Some of the wiser ones amongst us said, "No it is not a Hampden because it has a tail-gun to the rear".

Now a lad in the war years had to have a good knowledge of military aircraft, I suppose it was almost similar to the old days of the men quoting the Bible chapter and verse to one another. We lads were efficient at the plane spotting and we then noticed the crosses on the wings and shouted, "It's a Gerry". He did a bit of a dip and started to turn and we heard the crump crump of the bombs. The plane turned and came back over us, we lads were all yelling and swearing as it was the only weapons we had, then the sirens went and much to our disgust, we were all rushed to a shelter at the side of Two Steeples where Chitham's offices now stand and for a considerable time we were kept in this shelter. We were very upset that we had been put in a shelter when Gerry had gone.

After the "all clear", we came out and were told that because of the danger of Germans, the hike or trek was off, so we lads went down to Cavendish Road where we had heard the bombs had dropped. We were not allowed in the road, there was a soldier standing at the front of the road with a rifle and told us lads to get off, but we went round the back and found a little alley into a pub. We came back into Cavendish Road and destruction was everywhere. I remember a whole row of houses with its roofs sitting as if they had been lifted off on the road and an old woman dusting oranges, covered with glass and dust – it must have been early in the war years for oranges to be about.

Sometime before the end of the war I worked as a bicycle messenger for the Home Guard. A unit was stationed at Aylestone Lane and had their barricades at the Aylestone Lane Railway bridge. They slept in the old billiard hut at Uncle Les' yard. One day there were Home Guard manoeuvres and several of us Boy Scouts were given some training with carrier pigeons by Mr Middleton on Welford Road. We were shown how to write the message and place it in a little capsule which was then attached to the pigeon's leg.

The day of the manoeuvres was wet and we wore our bike capes to protect us from the elements. We were ordered by the Home Guard Officer, Mr Payne from Wigston Fields, to remove them. They were brilliant yellow and of course we could be seen for miles!

Suddenly advancing up the fields were several lines of men. Soldiers with rifles held in front of them. They came up the fields at a steady march. They made quite an imposing sight. At the footbridge ("Rally Bridge" to those who knew it well), another group became active, we were told to go and find out what was happening so we could send our message. The message duly written we lads said was wrong. Instead of the words "Enemy advancing in large numbers", we felt we should state

The hut on Aylestone Lane (owned by Les Forryan) which was used as a dormitory by the Home Guard during the Second World War, about 1948. The site is now occupied by offices but the hut now forms part of my museum.

The 2nd Platoon of the Wigston Magna Home Guard, about 1943. This platoon was responsible for guarding the railway and canal bridges in the area. At the front are (l-r): Rudkin, Crabtree, Tuckley, Hardy, Parker and Simpson. In the back row are (l-r): -?-, Biggs, Spence, -?-, Boulter, Savage, Skerritt, -?-, Foulston.

the exact number of the enemy, but we were soon told to obey orders and use the "official jargon".

We sent the pigeon off, forgetting in our excitement to check for overhead wires that were there, fortunately the pigeon missed the wires. We then went down to the bridge to see what was happening. Throwing discretion to the winds, we walked across and saw a large machine gun being mounted on a tripod. Fire-crackers started to go off, all hell broke loose. One of the local Home Guards who had got some blanks and had been itching to fire these off all day, slipped the first one "up the spout" of his rifle and banged away happily. Men appeared all around. A soldier wearing a white arm band with *umpire* on it and an agitated expression was shouting, "You bloody fools, you're shooting at your own side". Thank goodness it was only a practice!

Chapter Four

Wigston Folklore

The people of Wigston had many old sayings, remedies and superstitions which now seem to be forgotten. Therefore, I record here as many as I can remember.

REMEDIES

Old Mrs Hurst lived in Junction Road and was a great believer in onions as a curer of many, if not all, ills. If you had ear ache, you heated an onion up and held it against the ear; with tooth ache the onion went onto the tooth, and so on. She always had a peeled onion hanging in the house, every fortnight or so it was replaced with another onion. When the old onion was cut in half it would be black right through, this apparently proved that all disease had been taken out of the air. I believe she ate considerable quantities of onions as well.

Another old farming remedy got rid of boils. An old boy told how as a lad he had a lot of boils round his privates. The doctor could do nothing for him, but the old midwife, knowledgeable in these matters, gathered some cow dung as it fell. This she put onto his boils!

He declared he was in agony that night but in the morning every boil had been drawn!

The same type of cure was used for an abscess of the breast in women, here the midwife would use a cow dung poultice – primitive but it did the trick. It makes you shudder though!

My Aunt had diptheria when five years old. The doctor prescribed a toxin injection. My grandmother did not approve but asked the doctor if he would treat his child the same. He said he would, so the injection was given, but with no improvement and Aunt was dying. One day

Grandmother spoke to Mr Smith the blacksmith, who enquired of the family's health and was told the bad news. "Ar Mrs Forryan use the old cure" he said. "Get a shovel of hot coals and take it into the sick room, then sprinkle sulphur onto it". This was done and the fumes rose causing all and sundry to cough like mad. Aunty in a similar state coughed up a piece of tough skin, like leather. She improved from that point and lived another 60 years. Grandmother did not dare tell the doctor what she had done, so all parties were happy.

While we were carting corn we would also pick blackberries as we went down the hedgeside. We also gathered sloes to make sloe wine, crab apples to make beautiful crab apple jelly. Who can tell you where the crab apple trees of the district are now, who knows where violets can be found – not many!

Who can tell of the field which is a swamp wherein grow water Plantains?

It is fatal to let cattle or any pregnant animal graze in it because it causes abortions. It was said that the old miners' wives used to boil the water plantain leaves to make a mixture, so that when they had their many pregnancies, they could terminate some of them.

WEATHER LORE

These days when we are able to sit at home and watch the television weather forecast or ring up the recorded weather forecast to discover what the weather is going to be, we forget that years ago people had to rely on their local knowledge. In Wigston I can look at the sky and have a fair idea of what the weather is going to be. I utilise the old sayings which are perhaps not as accurate as modern forecasting, but nevertheless very useful. In a morning we used to say, "Rain before seven, fine before eleven". In the majority of cases this is still correct. We used to say "Three white (or hoar) frosts and then rain". This is not infallible, but late Autumn or early Spring seems to work this way.

"Candlemas Day bright and clear, two winters there will be this year". Candlemas Day is 2 February, and is the old half-way house of winter. At Candlemas Day you should have "Half your coal and half your hay". It seems that the weather pattern sets up at certain times of the year and Candlemas Day is one of these times and it is a reasonably accurate guide.

"February fill dyke black or white", as true now as the day it was first put into rhyme. So many of these old sayings are localised and come back to me at different seasons when the memory stirs of things. I was told as a lad. "Oak before the Ash we're in for a splash" – "Ash before the Oak we're in for a soak". "March comes in like a lamb out like a lion". "A quiet March borrows the first ten days of April".

An accurate one is "Fogs in March, frosts in May", if there is a fog on the 12th March, there is usually a frost on the 12th May!

An old saying familiar to all is "April showers bring forth May flowers". We then go to "May come early, May come late, May will make the old cow quake". So often in May we find we get cold snaps, but I feel here the May referred to is the May blossom and if the May blossom comes early or late, you get a cold snap somewhere about that time.

A pure farming adage goes, "When May is out sow barley day and night", also there is "Ne're cast a clout till May is out". This doesn't mean, as some of the old hands used to think, to stay sweating in woollen clothing in warm weather, but using it logically you will have cold weather in May. "A dripping June puts all things in tune" and when you think of it, although we curse rain in June it certainly helps along the young vegetables, plants and the crops. The alternative is also true: "Dry May good for corn but bad for hay".

"Two moons in May, no fruit, no flowers, no hay". One I learnt about thistles is "Mow them in June, you mow them too soon; mow in September, you've som'at to remember". Other general sayings are, "As the days lengthen, so the cold strengthens", and "Wash on New Year's Day, wash a life away".

The old saying "Raining on St Swithins it will rain for 40 days and 40 nights" is perhaps a little exaggerated but with rain on St Swithin's Day (15 July) you get an unsettled spell afterwards. "As the days lengthen so the cold strengthens" is often true, and a sure sign of the coming winter is "The ice in November to bear a duck, the next three months will be all sludge and muck".

There are many sayings to predict rain. The old warning "Red sky in the morning shepherd's warning, red sky at night shepherd's delight", is well known by all and is still a good guide. Others are "Mackerel sky not long wet, not long dry", or "Mackerel sky not three days dry", and "When the black slugs come out it will rain shortly". If cattle continue grazing it's only a short spell of rain, if they settle down a longer spell is nigh. If the Scarlet Pimpernel (flower) is open, nice weather – closed, rain is on the way. If cattle dance and skit about a weather change is nigh, wind usually.

"When the wind is in the East, it is neither good for man nor beast", is self-explanatory as the east wind brings us our extremes. The sailor would never sail on a Friday as the saying goes, "Wet Friday, wet Sunday, wet week" and the weather pattern usually does change on a Friday.

Once whilst we were hedge trimming a stout woman walking by ran or trotted for about ten yards and then resumed walking. "Rain about" said Uncle Les. "If you had asked that woman why she had run she couldn't tell you!" and it came on to rain.

"The old moon is the new moon's arms", is a sign of stormy weather and the new moon on its back will hold water, so a wet moon or lunar month is in prospect. A ring around the moon means frost.

DEALING WITH PROBLEMS

We were sometimes frightened as children if mother or father looked at the clock as bedtime approached and said, "Look at the time, the nine o'clock horses will have you!" What the horses were we did not know, but we were terrified and off we would shoot to bed. Some said that the horses were collecting the night soil from lavatory pits, not a pleasant sight, so it was done at night. The horses cast sparks from steel shoes on granite setts, plus the stink was enough to frighten anyone.

One of the tales I have heard through the years was of a dog that was a nuisance. An old boy said, "We scratched his arse with a pin and put some turps on, he ran for miles and wondered what had happened to him". I have heard of cats being a nuisance amongst the neighbour's pigeons, getting the same treatment. The cat would disappear at 900 miles an hour and not be seen for days. It must have been rather painful but effective.

At the village of Burton Overy, one old boy regularly got himself drunk, the lads of the village used to tease him unmercifully. One day he came out of the pub and the horse was in the shafts the wrong way round, the horse facing the cart. On another occasion they took the horse out of the cart, threaded the shafts through a gate and reharnessed the horse on the other side, another poser for him.

A tale comes to mind told to me by Les Forryan. He said that when he was in France in the First World War, some troops at rest discovered an orchard. There was an immediate scramble and a charge back to barracks with the apples. There were howls of disgust when the troops attempted to eat them because the apples were so bitter and sour, but Les, a countryman, had not gone mad and just taken the apples, he had tasted them first. It was a cider apple orchard with one or two eating apple trees interspersed between the cider apple trees. Les got the eating apples. He chuckled many a time in this telling of his yarn about the complaints of his fellow soldiers who were trying to eat such bitter fruit.

One often hears stories about wise old gentlemen or women who "knew better than the vet". We often credit such people with almost supernatural powers. But beware ! One day when I was a lad, I had a cow which "put its body out". The cow had calved and it had not cleansed properly. The cleansing (afterbirth to townees) was hanging down.

I asked an old boy what I should do, "Don't bother with the vet lad" he said, "tie a horse shoe on it!"

So I tied a horse shoe on the cleansing. When next I went in to see how the cow was faring, the poor animal was a gruesome sight. The "cure" was obviously not working, there was a horrible mass hanging out with muscles like lumps sticking over it.

Horrified, I immediately called the vet Mr Benbow. He chided me for my ignorance and said "Do not listen to some of these old wise boys, but get a sheet lad". Mother was most upset at the thought of a precious bed sheet being used. It was wartime and such things were strictly rationed. It would be very difficult to replace a damaged sheet. Anyway we got our sheet. One lad stood one side of the beast, and I stood on the other side supporting the body of the cow. Benbow lathered the protruding object all over with soap and water then gently eased it back into the cow. "Don't do it again lad", he said, "we've saved her for you and we won't kick your arse for you this time, but don't do it again!"

We got the old cow round and I had one of my object lessons.

Regrettably I did lose a cow that week because one died with a mortified calf inside her. When Uncle Les came back from holiday and I told him. He was a bit upset and made rather a hollow laugh. "Why do you laugh?", I enquired, surprised. He said, "Lad, while the cow is alive do your damnedest for it; when it is dead, why sit down and cry, you've got to laugh at these sorrows of life!"

GHOSTLY APPARITIONS

In August 1981 a woman and her son travelling from Nottingham to Basingstoke with a car and caravan, had the misfortune to break down. Her car needed two days to be repaired and they parked in fields called

Heards Close, opposite the Wigston Magna cemetery, to await the vehicle's return.

Mr Peter Wilford of the Wigston Historical Society spoke to her after her first night's stop and she told him of her fear of the site. "I'm psychic" she said, "and this is an evil spot. I heard shouts and shrieks, groans and clashing of metal, just as if a battle was being fought". Peter said nothing, wished her well and trusted she would sleep the second night. "I will", she said, "I've some strong sleeping pills".

Peter had previously found buried artefacts on the site, and so returned the following morning to speak again to the lady. "Did you sleep?" he asked. "Yes" was the reply, "but I was woken up by my son shouting 'get up, get up!'". Half awake the poor lady was confronted by a youth of pale countenance dressed in a white robe who then vanished. "My son was sleeping still in the bunk opposite totally unaware of our visitor", she said. Looking out of the caravan window the lady told Peter, "It was dawn and everywhere was covered in mist. Here's my car, I can't get away quick enough!" Peter never told of the facts he knew of regarding the area.

The Leicester Search Society, who have helped so much in investigating the area, has as its leader Mr Husgrove. His wife, without this knowledge, declared the area evil. She cannot explain her feeling but is very uncomfortable about the place when visiting her husband on his survey work.

Rowland, son of William Robinson, the gravedigger of the Welford Road Cemetery, told me that his father had found many artefacts in the area. These included a broken sword, and a smashed-in skull, surrounded by stones, pottery, beads, bits of harness and armour. He had told his son, "It was just as if a battle had taken place".

Mr William Ward an ardent Wigston historian, told me of a lady living in Homestead Drive who confided in him one day, saying – "Bill I've had a vision, I saw men in ancient costume, mediaeval armour". The lady asked Bill to accept her confidence again as she thought no one would believe her. When Bill reassured her she continued – "As I looked out of the kitchen window towards the cemetery it was misty and an army or large numbers of men with spears and shields and armour were walking or marching through the mist, but then they were gone as quickly as they had appeared".

Very recently, a couple and their daughter chose to walk home to Wigston Harcourt the long way around after an evening at the

Navigation Inn, Kilby Bridge. They walked along the tow path beside the canal and then up and over the railway and on to Cooks Lane. While on the stretch leading to Norwood House, the couple noticed a vague, grey misty figure cross in front of them. It apparently wore a cloak and had something protruding or trailing at one side, like a sword. Their daughter asked if they had noticed anything and then complained she had seen a greyish-white figure with a child or some object under a misty type of cloak.

Is there a message coming to us from this ancient spot? We know this area has been inhabited since prehistoric times. Was this area the site of the original Wigston?

Was it later destroyed and the settlement rebuilt in the Two Steeples area?

Chapter Five

Working Wigston

During my childhood, there were still many of the traditional craftsmen and traders working in Wigston. Here are some recollections of a few of them.

"Kilby" Clark, a wheelwright, had his woodyard at the top of Kilby village. He also had a yard at Wigston opposite the "Two Steeples", later Mansfield Hosiery factory. He built himself a house which still stands, it is a flat roofed house today partly used by a car trimming firm.

The yard started with the paint shop. His paints were made from a lead base with varying pigments and the farm vehicles derived their pretty and bright colours, so he told me, from the dyes in the ground. On the wall in the paint shop was an old board which for many years he had used to clean his brushes and it was thick with layers of paint. He said he had been offered a lot of money by someone who wanted to plane it lightly to show a rainbow effect and make a picture of it.

Next came the blacksmith's shop. There was a forge in one corner with huge bellows and as full an array of shoeing blacksmith's equipment as one could wish for. The last shoeing smithy in Wigston was at the Bell Inn. The smith, O'Connor by name, lived down Wigston Fields. He was the last smith to be employed by the railway company. He did his shoeing casually for the few farm horses left in Wigston in an afternoon. Uncle Les played hell with me when it cost £1 to have the last horse we had shod and he swore he would never have another horse shod as inflation was too rampant. It is quite common now to pay £20 to have a riding horse shod.

The Smith family's smithy, Bull Head Street, 1904. Mr Mayling stands
with "Mark Anthony", a horse from Wigston Hall. The site was
demolished in the 1950s and is now occupied by the Heron Garage.

Clarkes had an assortment of tools for other blacksmithing work, such
as making wheels and various ironworks for carts. He used to tell me that
cartwheel tyres were made up of strips of metal some 18 inches long,
which were bent into rough shape and linked to form the tyre.

I did once help to put a tyre on a wheel for Mr Clarke. A fire was lit
and the iron rim was heated, the wheel which had been made previously
by him lay on the floor. The iron rim expanded when hot and was
lowered over the wheel, as soon as it was on, water was poured on it to
cause the metal to cool and contract, thereby binding tight onto the
wooden wheel, for good measure spikes were driven through the tyre into
the wooden wheel to secure it.

Sometimes, coming downhill with a horse and cart, we would drag
the wheel against the kerb to act as an additional brake. It was effective,
but when as sometimes happened, this tactic fetched the tyre off we

The Hallam family of tree fellers, 1920s.

really got into trouble. In dry weather we would soak the wagon wheels with water so that the wood would swell again and hold tight against the iron rim.

In the woodshop proper where a tree would arrive, an old gas engine drove all the machinery, there were pulleys and rollers, band saws, rip saws, all sorts. The tree entered here and exited as logs or planks. There were open barns in which to dry the timbers.

There was a sawpit here before Clarke acquired his machinery. This was simply a pit similar to an inspection pit in a garage with rollers on it. The tree was dragged on to it and a man stood on top holding the old fashioned cross-cut saw with 'T' shaped handle, he was the guide man. A man underneath, called the Bottom Man, would follow the saw along under the guidance of the man above. The term "Top Dog" applied to the top man on the saw pit. They had to work as a team and it must have been a rotten job being the bottom man. All the muck and sawdust dropped on you.

Wheelwright Clarke told me how "miserable devils from the Council" stopped him from bringing trees into his workshop. I asked why they should do this. Apparently he used a huge pair of wheels – Ginny

Men's work at the Two Steeples factory: knitting vests, 1925.

Wheels – which straddled the tree. The tree was jacked up by the use of huge jacks and fantastically long spanners some three to four feet long. The tree was then fastened under the axle of the ginny wheels and secured. Horses were hooked on to the tree and towed it with the butt trailing on the ground. When they went downhill men would sit on the butt, causing it to drag on the ground and act as a brake. You can imagine the effect of this on the roads, no wonder the Council stopped it! He also told me that Gimsons had a pair of huge ginny wheels measuring six feet high to the axle, what fantastic wheels they must have been!

I remember trees being felled in the Memorial Park by I believe Hallams a Wigston family of tree fellers. They worked as a beautifully smooth team, one each end of the cross cut saw, zip, zip and through the tree it went. I have used this method myself with Ernie Munton when we cleared a hedge out on some land I bought from Jimmy Gee. Although I was a very young man at the time, it was certainly hard work and unless

Women's work at the Two Steeples factory: sewing garments, 1925.

the two cutters worked perfectly as a team it was real hard graft. The saw had to be kept keenly sharp as there was no motor to flog it out as we do today.

Clarke's yard was a paradise to me and many others. A fine museum was lost to Wigston for a mere £10! Just before old wheelwright Clarke died, he did a job for me costing £10. I had not got the £10 at the time to pay, so I went round to pay his widow a little later. There was a scrapman, fetching everything away and I expressed surprise. Mrs Clarke said, "Sorry lad I needed the money". It's a shame that the people in Wigston hadn't foresight to see the value of preserving these old tools of a fast disappearing trade. It is to my lasting regret, that if I had not been tight for a tenner, I could perhaps have saved them from being scrapped.

Mr Clarke built quite a few houses in Wigston. He is mentioned in the Congregational Chapel minutes when he did work for them. Other builders in Wigston were Southams, Lowes and Smiths. They had their hand trucks on which materials were placed and pushed around the district. Scouts used to borrow one of these trucks and some would be in front pulling and others at the back also with a rope hanging on when the truck went down hill. It was the ambition of the scouts to have a trek cart. My troop (the old 28th) never did achieve this goal and relied on the builders for the loan of their cart.

Old wheelwright Clarke was a builder, wheelwright, blacksmith, as well as a painter. You name it, he would do it. He once made a wheel for a watermill, with the help of Gary Phillips of Leicester Road. The wheel was a masterpiece in craftmanship, and with its wooden teeth it was a reflection on this versatile man. What a change from today when our technology dictates a narrow course for individuals to take in life. He cursed most angrily about these new fangled metal things, which had driven the old craftsmen out of business. Shades of today, when everyone is frightened of modernisation, perhaps rightly.

BUTCHERY

Bell Street corner was quite an event when a slaughtering took place. The cattle would have been in the fasting pen over the weekend and sometimes, if it was a noisy beast, there was one hell of a rumpus from the neighbours, "Them ruddy Forryan's and their cattle, what a din!" But they didn't go to the Public Health Inspectors in those days, it was an albeit noisy part of life.

The shutters would be shut on the house and the beast was driven down the yard to slaughter. The beast went into a narrow pen at the end of the slaughter house. Through a door at the side someone would drop a noose over the horns of the animal (most cattle were horned at that time, the sophistication of "poling" cattle -that is removing the horns by artificial means or scientific breeding- had not been introduced).

The beast had to be pulled down to its knees so that it could be pole-axed. Children coming from school used to gather around and hang up on the rope helping to pull the beast down. There was a ring in the floor through which the rope was pulled. When the beast was on its knees and was hit quite smartly with a sharp wallop with the pole-axe it would pierce the skull. To make sure the animal was dead, the brain was stirred or poked with a stick. The beast was then hung up by its hind legs and the skinning and dressing took place. The blood ran into a pit and was saved, either for use on the gardens, or for making into black pudding.

The killing of pigs was quite an art. I witnessed more of this at

Freckingham's in Long Street, although I did see some slaughtering take place in Bell Street. A pig was held and shot with a humane killer, the carcass was then lifted quickly onto the "scratch", which was a low wooden thrall with two handles at each end for moving it around. The pig was then "stuck" in the throat to bleed. The copper would be boiling merrily. A huge wooden tub was pushed alongside the scratch and filled with water. The water temperature was critical, the pig was then dipped in and the slaughterers got busy with their scrapers.

If the water was not hot enough the hair would not come off. If it was too hot it would start to cook the skin and instead of just the hair coming off the skin would come with it and someone would get cursed. They took a pride in not leaving one hair on the body when a pig was scraped. The body was then hoisted up and someone with a very, very sharp knife, would quickly run over it to trim any hair that the scrapers' had missed.

We used to enjoy this, we even enjoyed watching them being gutted, but one thing that did make us squirm was when the scraper was reversed. On the other end of the scraper was a small hook used to hook off the toes of the pig's trotters!

I never saw a lamb shot. Lambs were killed by having their throat cut and bled, then the skinning took place. There was very little refrigeration in those days, although there was a chill room in which the meat was stored. Prior to that everything killed had to be eaten during that week before if went 'off'. What a problem it must have been in hot weather.

TRAVELLING TRADERS

I remember the old mushroom men who passed through the village in the autumn at eventide with huge skeps on their backs, they spent the night under a haystack or any farm building available. When dawn arrived they were up and scouring the fields for their mushroom harvest and we should see them returning to Leicester as we went to work.

The hot tripe man used to come somewhere from the direction of Kilby or Arnesby on his float and shouting, "Hot tripe!". But having helped in the slaughterhouses seeing the tripe in its raw state, I have never been able to face it. Neither could I face "chitterlings" or pigs guts after seeing them turned inside out to be cleaned.

Chirper Vann who lived up Leicester Road often had his very old motor bike loaded up with rabbits and the front of his shop always seemed to have rabbits on sale. A poor man's food but I still think it is a tasty dish as any. I also remember the weekly visit of the barrel organ and the rag and bone man who gave squares of salt in exchange for rags.

THE NECESSITIES OF LIFE

Sewage from Kilby Bridge was pumped into a tanker which was pulled by horse, which was then tipped into the sewer along Welford Road. For a consideration it could be emptied onto a farmer's land. I am not sure whether it was Horace or Arthur Wormleighton who was said to have been on the cart eating dinner, while carrying a full load. In those days men didn't stop for dinner as they do now, and he said to his mate, "Stop stirring that with your finger, I am eating my dinner!" His colleague replied, "So am I, but I have lost my cheese"!

Such was the humour about anything.

People were always to be seen ambling round the fields "sticking" for firewood. Mrs Chamberlain would always have her bags full of sticks. "Stickers" loved storms because they broke nice little chunky bits of branch from the Ash trees. One old dear, when I called in, had the line prop in the room, one end was in the fire, the other end on a stool. As it burned she "hotched" the stool along to move the prop into the fire – "Good old days"!

I believe my aunt Gladys Forryan was the last sticker in Wigston. When she became too old to work, we brought sticks and logs for her.

The stickers were useful to us farmers because if anything was wrong such as a sheep on its back, or a horse cut with barbed wire, we were immediately told. Mushrooms as well as sticks went into the bag of course and watercress too was a favourite "crop".

The Great Wigston Gas Company was one of the village's earlier firms, founded in 1856. The coal was supplied by the old firm of Eli Bailey. The Baileys carted coal in Wigston for over a century. Eli Bailey had Lodge Farm along the Aylestone Lane. When I was a lad his son Jack farmed there. He later farmed the Goldhill and Shackerdale Farms, before they were finally gobbled up by the builders. The connection between the Baileys and the Gas dated from time immemorial. Baileys carted the coal from South Wigston station up over Spion Kop to the Gas Works in Newgate End. The man who did the bulk of this work with the horse was named Jack Whale. He had a very tall horse called

Ginger, and Ginger used to "step along". Prior to working with the Baileys, Jack had a small-holding up Cooks Lane, but it was uneconomical. He was the last person to live in the old and now defunct spring cottage in Cooks Lane. A new house is now on the site.

Jack's task was to go up the Aylestone Lane on his bike in the summer, catch his horse which was in the field (in the winter he would fetch it from the stable) then he would harness it, put it in the cart, walk it all the way down to Wigston Magna along Long Street and down Station Road, throw on out of the rail wagon some 35 cwts of coal, walk over Spion Kop to the gasworks, tip it, ride back, do six loads a day and then take his horse back up to Bailey's, untackle it, rub it down, feed it and make his way home. What a day's work, day in, day out!

I can't recollect Jack ever being ill.

Sometimes he would bring two horses. This would be a great day because it meant he would pump the tar out of the pit at the gasworks, take it with the two horses in tandem down to South Wigston railway sidings to be moved by rail. We had one of Bailey's old horses named "Smiler". She was possibly one of the most powerful horses that ever walked and one of the most idle!

They used to let her pull the tar wagon on her own because she would not pull if another horse was there and would bust a weaker horse. Old Smiler had "greasy heels", this caused irritation and itching which must have been unbearable for the horse. Alongside the railway embankment by Lodge field, was a strip of land belonging to the railway and fenced off with iron railings. Smiler went the whole length of these railings in a short time, itching and kicking, and she literally kicked them into knots of twisted metal.

If when we were haymaking and sweeping the hay, we should cut across short as we call it, and the chain on the harness touched Smiler's fetlock, she would lash out immediately and bang would go the chain. We used to carry a hammer in one pocket and a splitlink in the other to repair the chain. It was quite a work of art to keep her off her chains. Uncle Les had a terribly sore face once, an infection that was caught from the horse's sore fetlocks.

Another familiar sight was of Mr Proctor and Mr Vann pushing round a truck in which they had collected gas meter money. This was mainly in pennies and was quite a considerable weight. The truck was a very narrow one with iron wheels and arching handles. They had to put great effort into pushing it around the district, stopping and paying it in at the Midland Bank, Long Street.

Milk delivery by motorcycle; Mr Burnett of Sutton in Elms, 1930s. I
delivered much milk in Wigston by the same means until the 1950s.

Over the years I have seen many forms of transport used in Wigston. I
remember seeing the "gentry" going to Church on Sunday in their
carriage and pair of horses, the Owston's of Bushloe House with Ted
Harold with the reins and Mortlocks of Abington with Alan Boniface in
the driving seat. They drove up in style with their open landau in
summer or closed landaulette in bad weather.

Motorbikes and sidecars were used tremendously. Chipper Vann used a
motorbike for his rabbit and game shop, as did Mr Bradshaw of the
Hardware shop in Leicester Road. Billy Cartwright the village chimney
sweep, who lived in Leicester Road had one. As a lad I can well
remember asking, "Who is that man?" and my mother replying, "It's
Cartwright", but I said, "He is a black man"!

On this occasion Billy was dressed very smart with his face and hands
clean, it was the first time I could recollect seeing Billy Cartwright with his
face clean.

The Bank, looking east from Bell Street, 1920s. This was Wigston's main bus terminus.

My own combination was known in the village for the Collie bitch I owned. She would stand in my sidecar. My first motorbike was a 1927 AJS and when the cylinder head gasket kept blowing, I got fed up and ran it without one. It was rather noisy but still remarkably efficient. I would come down the street, the dog barking (it wouldn't stop however much I hit it) and the motorbike pop, popping, and they said they knew when Duncan was coming. Good job I wasn't a poacher!

There was one character who had a motorbike and sidecar. This sidecar was not very large and was pointed at the front almost like a coffin. This person had to fetch an old ewe which was very ancient and was kept solely to keep the tup company in the summer. When he got there he was told that a milk churn had to be taken back as well. Now how did he you get a ewe and a churn in a sidecar? He sat the ewe on its haunches and stuck the churn in front of it. What a sight it must have been!

It's many years since we saw the arrival of bus transport for the village, the first bus service was by the old A.B.C. company run by the three Beasley brothers, Bill, Bob and Bert, along with their sister Flo who acted as conductor. This company started in 1920 with solid tyred, open topped London buses. Another service was started by Jacky Wallace of

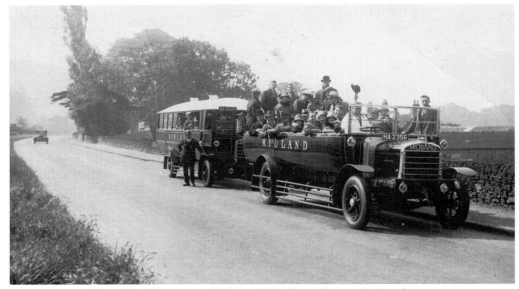

Midland Red buses at work, late 1920s. Here a bus and a charabanc are taking employees of the Wigston Co-Operative Society on an excursion to the Peak District.

Shearsby with his "Pilot" bus service and also by Shirley Snutch of Arnesby. These two were originally country carriers but expanded into a bus service and were eventually taken over by the "Midland Red". We had at this time our own three village carriers, George Dawson, George Scotcher and Charlie Wright, who ran daily services into Leicester. Previous to this we had Henry Poyner running his old model T. Ford open tourer car but his trip finished at Clarendon Park tram terminus and the journey into Leicester being completed by tram car. His fare was 6d and he would have done well in a sardine factory, how he managed to pack his passengers in.

At that time bus fares were cheap, 4d single and 7d return, while the fare from Wigston Bank to Canal Street was 1d. This was useful for those going to South Wigston pictures which at that time were shown in the old Clarence Hotel. The show was run by Mr Smith and silent films were the order of the day with music provided by Perce Rowley on the piano and Horace Stevens on the violin. At that time we had no picture house in Wigston.

Chapter Six
Agricultural Wigston

*Today Wigston is very much an industrial town, with large
residential areas adjoining Leicester. It is hard to imagine therefore,
that only 50 years ago, agriculture pervaded so much of village life.*

As a child, I kept rabbits and hens, dug my patch of the garden, grew
vegetables and learnt the art of getting eggs from a broody hen. I was
taught how to kill and pluck birds; to test if a hen was in lay by the
width of its vent bones; how to dress the perches with nicotine to kill the
b——y fleas; how to break and wring a hen's neck and that if you pluck
it before it stops kicking you don't tear the flesh.

I also bred rabbits, showed them, and killed, skinned and ate them,
cured the skins or sold them for 10d each. At the age of eleven I had a
morning and evening paper round – five bob a week. On Saturdays I
delivered meat for Uncle Ernie prior to garage work.

I left school at the age of fifteen and began my life working on the
land. I started farming at the age of 21 with 12 acres, after building up a
bit of cash and stock on my allotment. I worked part-time for my Uncle
Les and used to assist with the threshing. I wasn't paid but took corn in
lieu of cash, the idea being to feed corn to my poultry and stock and
build it up that way. Regrettably, I had my poultry stolen the first
Christmas!

AGRICULTURAL TERMS

We had different names for things. We would "stook the corn", or
"stouck the corn". We had yellow weed charlock or "chadlock", or
"cadlock", depending whereabouts you were. I was talking to a

Welshman who had lived nearly all his life in Leicestershire, and he told of when he came to the village of Owston with his dog as a lad, the farmer, Mr Guildford, said to him, "Right you have got your dog, go into this field and show me what you can do". So he rounded up the sheep and examined them and the farmer said, "Anything wrong?" "Yes" he said, "they have got fly". When he was asked if he had finished this shepherding job and he replied "Yes", "What about the cattle?" he was asked. Shepherding in Wales is sheep, and cattle are something different. But here in Leicestershire looking after stock, any type of stock, is always referred to as "shepherding".

One day, I was sent to Charley Harrison at the old Shackledale farm to fetch some seed corn. I was asked, "How many strikes do you want?" – or strykes. A stryke of corn was a bushel measure of volume and was used before they had scales. If you heap up above the sides of any object and then smooth it level by using a straight rod, you have struck it level; corrupt to strike. Some of the old hands used to call a sheaf of corn a "stryke".

PLOUGHING

In Wigston dialect, ridge and furrow is pronounced as "rig and turrow". In many fields it was very noticeable and there are still examples around the village. Each ridge was a man's strip which he ploughed or dug. He got more land out of the same space by throwing his soil to the centre and over the years produced a corrugated effect on the field's surface; more land in the same space with a natural drainage running off from the top of the ridge. The furrow acted as drainage.

Most of these ridges were a furlong long and had a slight curve at each end like a modest 'S'. This was where the oxen used to start their swing to pull out. With modern ploughing if you try and cut the corner and not set square each time, you get this 'S' in the set out. When tractors were first used, if your furrows weren't straight, you had your leg pulled; a darn good incentive to get quality in work.

To get into the fields of Wigston, there were no permanent roads and a headland used to be made, which was a huge ridge and this used to weave its way through the fields. Many modern roads were built on top of these weaving headlands and hence the weaving English road.

On the ends of some of the ridges you will see an unusual knob, this is where the old wooden ploughs were cleaned. Mud sticking to the wooden

A good straight furrow; the view from Vin Wilford's tractor during
ploughing, 1940s.

plough mould boards would have caused a drag and they had to be cleaned
at the end of the furrows – the evidence remains. One can also note in some
instances that the hedges were laid when the land was enclosed and so cut
across the ridge and furrow. Also, along the side of the canal or the railway,
can be seen the banks where they cut up the old layouts.

Before the enclosure of Wigston's fields in 1764 there were a lot of
cereals grown, with grazing on common land and headlands. But
afterwards, and until 1939, there were strong terms against ploughing
up the leased land. A fine of £20 per acre was imposed if any grass land
was ploughed up in 1856.

THE CORN HARVEST

Corn harvesting was one of the great occasions when everyone worked
together. My first experience of this was when we started mowing the

"Long Field" (West Avenue). There we went with our scythes and I was told we had got to mow a road round, otherwise the tractor would knock too much corn down. Uncle Les and old Bert Rudkin were swishing away with the scythe cutting the corn and leaving it in a swath. We lads were shown how to tie up sheaves using the corn itself as a band. These sheaves were laid in the hedge-side and then the binder followed on the cleared track and we would stack the corn. For this we brought the sheaves we had hand-tied back into the field and forming a stook, along with the machine cut sheaves.

A stook consisted of six or eight sheaves which were stood together in a double row with the heads touching and the butts standing out to leave an inverted V through which the air could blow and dry the corn. The cart or wagon went between the rows with pitchers on each side who would pitch the sheaves onto the cart. A good pitcher could throw the sheaves accurately, placing them so that the loader had virtually nothing to do but "bind his middle". That is, lay sheaves in the middle of the load so they supported the outside ones.

As it came out of the binder the sheaf had a slight angle on it. If you walked up behind the sheaf with the heads away from you, you could pick them up, flip one neatly under each arm and bring them smartly together down at the stooks and bed them pretty solidly. What a terrible job it was after a storm when the sheaves and stooks were blown over, we had to restook twisted ones. If you were stooking barley the whiskers would stick into your arms and make them very sore. The many thistles were hell. Sometimes the thistles were so bad we used to stand the sheaves up with pitch forks.

When the sheaves were carted to the stack, the stackers flipped each sheaf so that it lay at a slight angle and formed the wall. The middle was kept high, each sheaf projecting out, the stack wall had a slight outward lean which threw the rain clear. As soon as was possible when the heat had gone from the stack it would be thatched. I never did any house thatching, but plenty of corn rick thatching.

One year it was so wet that the corn grew in the stooks and we had to pick up the whole stook as the sheaves would not separate. As we built the stack we kept a large straw-filled sack in the centre which was pulled up as we worked, thus leaving a vent or chimney. This allowed the heat generated by the wet and growing corn to escape. When this stack was finished it would settle as the heat – as steam – escaped. When we threshed it the sheaves were pressed into wafers and crikey how the dust flew!

A stook of corn made up of tied sheaves, with John Rawson behind,
1940s.

Threshing corn, 1950s.

After threshing all the team had headaches and nausea which felt like sledge hammers on the head and horses kicking the guts in. Once I found ashes at the bottom of the vent. The stack heat had caused internal combustion but for some reason it had fired and gone out. The Good Lord was kind to me, as the stack was not insured.

Before threshing we would put wire netting around the stack and up to the threshing drum. When we threshed we would catch all the vermin. During these operations teams of men and women would work together and this is where some of the old comradeship and yarning would take place (which has been lost) and which is the main source of the tales and rambled yarns I attempt to tell here.

HAYMAKING AND STACKING

My first experience of earning farming money was along with my cousin Norman. We went to help Uncle Les, Ernie Bradshaw and some others make hay. "Can we help you?", we asked. "Sure lads, get those forks and rakes, keep clearing up". The hay was being brought in with the horse, collected with the hay sweep.

A sweep was made from a beam of wood some seven feet long, with slightly sharpened tynes stretching forward some two or three feet. There were two handles that came up at the rear held by the the man at the back. The horse pulled this along with a chain attached at each end. As the horse walked up the windrow (the row that was raked together from the swath, the swath being a strip of mown grass), care had to be taken. If you left the handles too high the point of the sweep dug in the ground and horse would roll the sweep straight over and away from you.

At the same time, the horse was controlled by plough lines. If you were doing your job properly you got the sweep full of hay. You then returned to the stack and stopped the horse. Digging in the tynes, "get up!" you would shout, and over would go the sweep and you would leave the hay there ready for pitching onto the stack.

If the hay was not fit enough for stacking, we made it into cobs. These

A haysweep at work on the Wild family's farm at Hambleton, Rutland, 1920s. Similar sweeps were used in Wigston.
(Rutland County Museum collection)

Looking north up Newgate End, about 1900. Note the fine thatched haystack in the middle of the foreground.

were in the shape of an upturned egg cup without the stem. We built small cobs all over the field and built in the same principle as a stack – only round. Here the pitchers had to lay the hay on, so we usually put a small boy on top to trample it down. The pitchers laid the hay delicately with the forks and yet with speed, so that the hay flopped over and allowed the rain to run off. The hay could cure in the cobs with the wind whistling round them. When the weather was fit and the hay had cured, it was carried to the stack.

Building a stack is a skilled craft. The art of putting a hay stack up was to get a good, a dry base of straw, brash, anything that was dry and was spare and not edible, then start the haystack on it. The corners were marked out in hay and then the walling commenced. The centre was always kept well full, the reason being that if rain got into the stack it would spoil. The full centre would tend to shed the rain out. Loose hay had to be laid and shaken out into the stack, so that the bulk of the grass straws or grasses formed like a thatched effect.

If the hay was stacked too early it could heat up and internal combustion might occur and what a black mark that would be to the farmer in the neighbourhood, because it was reckoned it was damned bad farming. Once the stack settled it had to be pulled. You stood alongside the stack and you pulled the loose hay off to give it a very firm finish. This made the sides almost impervious to rain, but what a job it was when you had thistles in the stack! The stack was then ready for thatching.

For this we used the battens of straw which had come from the threshing machine. This was raked into bundles roughly with a comb (invariably an old broken axe handle with six-inch nails driven through). These bundles were called "yelmes", which formed a layer of the thatch. About six or seven of these were laid one on top of the other diagonally, and tied in with a rope and passed to a man on the stack. He laid the bundles on one after the other, and then combed the whole lot down to give a constant thatch. These he held down by means of hazel, willow, or elm pegs, which he pushed firmly into the stack with string between the pegs.

When I had my first go at thatching old Mr Wilford came up to me and said, "Duncan have you seen all those blind sparrows bumping into things?" He said, "That thatching you did, the bits you left sticking up are blinding all the sparrows". I felt very embarrassed, but my uncle did save me by saying, it was better to have blind sparrows than no thatching like some people he knew, looking directly at my accuser who sometimes did not bother to thatch, indicating the pride of farmers.

Some stacks were round, some half-round, some square and some rectangular, a tremendous variety existed to suit all customs and areas. It was said that a man could go anywhere in England and tell where he was in whatever county, by the shape of the thatch and the stack. They were definitely very distinct. The hay stack was hard graft, hard work, but there was a great pleasure in the achievement of putting up a good stack and skill in curing your hay. Hay was cut from the stack with a hay knife. This was a huge blade with a wooden handle at the right angle on top kept razor sharp to ease the hard graft of cutting solid hay. It was cut into squares or trusses, loaded onto the dray or cart, roped down and carted. What a job this was in a gale!

One very wet year, which left the stack black, my Uncle Arnold told me to put it in the middle of the field. His advice was, "Let the beasts help themselves. If they're pinching it they will eat it, in any case they would sooner eat that than their own front legs!".

A haystack in the shape of a cottage is only a memory now. It was ideal for children to play in, adults to make love in, or, as often happens to ricks near to a town, providing an easily lit bonfire. I well remember leaving the Second Field (an area now occupied by Carlton Drive) with a load of hay. I had just arrived at Les Forryan's farm with my load when a breathless child on a bike raced up to me, "Your hay stack's on fire Mister". Sure enough some children had set fire to the stack. The firemen and I cut the stack, to stop the fire and I ended that day very wet, very black, very angry and extremely tired. I have fought two other stack fires since then, one of which was in a dutch barn, all caused by careless children. Around Wigston the hay stacks were built especially high, to prevent kids getting on.

MANGLES

To grow mangles we sowed mangle wurzle on top of the ridges produced by ridge ploughing. In Wigston we used to put in a mixture of lettuce, carrot,

Digging mangles from a clamp on Pickard's Farm, Ragdale, 1896.
(Leicestershire Record Office, Henton Collection)

turnip, swede, beetroot, raddish, any root vegetable. The amazing thing was that we grew lettuce up to 7lbs. beside a great big mangle wurzle.

Mr Thornhill who once lived in Cook's Lane used a precision method to sow mangles. He screwed bobbins on to each heel and walking along with one foot close to the other in a straight row, this would leave a hole and his wife would follow behind him dropping seed into each.

Mangle wurzle never suffered during a drought as the tap root went deep down. It seemed to shield and protect other plants. You could pull up a magnificent carrot alongside one, remarkable when you think that if you don't single your carrots you get poor crops. But our backs would ache after hoeing away on very heavy soil at Aylestone Lane. We were always told, "You are too young to have back ache", we didn't agree. Any excuse to stand up and sharpen the hoe, which would itself make the work easier.

One never used the hands in singling at all if possible, push and pull on the hoe and thin out the plants that you didn't want by the corner or the back of the hoe. The plants were left between nine and twelve inches apart. Cutting off the mangle was another tough job. Mangles were part of the farming year, sowed in May, hoed and singled before haymaking started, hoed when haymaking was finished, pulled after harvest. We didn't start mangle pulling until the October Fair, -the first week in October. That was the day the tupps were put with the ewes.

The pulling often took place in the bad weather. On a cold frosty morning, the job was very hard going: bare hands holding a mangle, tugging it up, putting it across your knee, scraping the mud off the root with the back of a long knife, and then cutting under the leaves in a way that left you holding the leaves while slinging the root into a heap. You finally dropped the leaves on another heap ready to cover up. Sometimes your hands would be so cold and wet that you didn't feel a cut. But when the hand thawed a bit and the juice of the mangle went into the cut, then you really knew to it! My hands (and those of all mangle pullers) are well scarred with cuts.

The roots were then covered in heaps with the leaves in rows with room for a cart between them. The cart would be brought down the rows, the roots were uncovered, the leaves scattered because they would scour the cattle if eaten and were best ploughed in. Then the roots were thrown into the cart. Woe betide you if one went over the cart and hit your mate at the back of the head. The cart would be loaded and brought back to the farm and the phase "shoulder to wheel" really came into play.

You leaned on the wheel as the horse backed up, then pushed the cart back up the ruts, tipping the load ready to be clamped.

The mangle clamp would be something like seven feet high and the outside had the form of an inverted 'V'. This would then be strawed and six to nine inches of soil put on the straw with gaps just left along the top for the warmth from the mangle to get out.

All this work with the mangle was done by hand. In the winter they were fetched out for the cattle to feed on, then a fork could be used. Here again more sweat took place, as you churned by hand the old mangle pulper which shredded the mangle up. Prior to that a crude cutting tool was used to chop them up. This had a cross-shaped blade but care had to be used with this as it was injurious for the cattle if the mangle was not properly cut up.

MILKING

When I dress for work, the first thing I do is roll up my shirt sleeves and this comes from the old hand-milking days. When I went into a cow shed in the morning, it was always warm inside. Off would come your coat, your sleeves would be rolled up and under the cow you would sit, head in the flank. You always wore a cap to prevent the fleas getting into your hair. You would sit on the right hand side of the cow, with your right hand towards the cow's head. After washing the cow's udder, you would sit down on the little stool, with one leg round the bucket in the front and one at the back with the bucket held firmly between the knees and start milking.

When you try this for a start it is darned hard work, but once you get used to it you develop muscles on your forearms and a tremendous strength in the wrist. This does not mean that you put strength behind milking, it is quite a skill and if you squeeze too hard, wham! the cow will kick. To stop it kicking, as you sit with the head in the flank you feel the foot coming up, you just stick your left arm out and hold the leg away, letting the kick come over the wrist – after you have had a kick or two in the guts you certainly make sure that you can do that.

In the summer, if the cows got a few tags of muck on their tail and caught you one on the ear, when flicking flies off themselves, the sting was terribly painful. This was another reason for wearing a cap on the head and the head in the flank. You could wedge the cow's tail between your head and the flank to stop it flicking. If the muck on the tail was wet you used to get a beautiful pattern of cow muck on your face!

My self-built cow shed at White Gate Farm, 1960s. This is now used as a farm shop.

A tale my old Uncle Les used to laugh at, was of a young lad who used to come round to the sheds in Bell Street. Young lads used to wear frocks until they were about five years old, but this lad's parents were keeping him longer in frocks than usual. He was standing watching the milking when the accident happened, a cow coughed and dunged at the same time. The effect was dramatic, the poor lad was smothered from head to toe and his parents never attempted to wash the frocks, they just dumped them and the lad went into trousers from then on.

It used to be great fun when the cat walked into the cowshed and we sprayed it with milk. The cat soon got very adept and would sit and catch the squib of milk in its mouth. After milking we would strain the milk, cool it, put it into buckets and deliver the stuff on our bikes. The regular run used to be with two three-and-a-half-gallon buckets of milk on each handle bar. A sack on the handle bar used to prevent the buckets from slipping on the metal. We had a crate on the front to carry some bottles and often we would carry eggs as well whenever they were available. Rather a precarious load but rarely a spill.

DROVING

Cattle were still driven through the streets of Wigston up to 1950. Very large herds of fat cattle from the Peats, farmers of Foston, used to be driven to Leicester Cattle Market for slaughtering. What fun when they charged their own reflections in a shop window or barged up an entry and indulged in a merry dance around some unfortunate back garden!

There was an old drover I used to yarn with when I worked up at Les Forryan's Farm. He lived in "China Town" -the Saffron Lane Estate. When he became a drover and was driving his herd or flock down Bell Street, he would knock on the King William pub window and shout his order to the landlord. He would then go and turn his charges into Aylestone Lane, leave them with the two or three dogs he had and return to the King William to have his glass, or jar, of ale and some bread and cheese. Not perhaps the luxury meal we now call quaintly a Ploughman's lunch, but basically of course the same. He would return to his herd after his repast and continue on to Leicester.

My droving work was to bring the cows on either the old footroad field which is now the Recreation ground against the Willow Park, or the second field which was on the opposite side of the lane and take them to the old farm buildings against the railway bridge for milking. I had these cattle very well trained, I would fetch them on my bike and would walk them along one side of the road so that the traffic (which was considerably lighter in volume than it is today) could get by them.

One of the cows that used to lead was the queen of the herd called Matilda, she had a huge udder which used to swing and nearly touch the floor after her calving. Our milk round was in Northfield Avenue and Aylestone Lane and the women customers used to shout "bring ours from that one Duncan". Nowadays it would be a nightmare to attempt to drove cattle up Aylestone Lane!

Mr Hoskins, late of Norwood House, Cooks Lane, was a farm labourer at Foston, and he drove large herds through Wigston. He has vivid memories of some episodes including the time a steer, or bullock, ran away from the herd. It went up an entry at the side of the 'King William' and jumped over a wall. Bullocks aren't built for steeplechasing and it split its aitchbones. The poor beast had to be left where it lay because the men could not leave the herd. Masons, the knacker men from Cooks Lane, had to come and put it down.

Cattle being driven down the High Street, Market Harborough, about 1897. (Harborough Museum collection)

HORSES AND TRACTORS

When leading the horses through mud, driving reins were always used. If you held onto the bridle, you would get absolutely splattered up as the great hooves stamped down into the mud to get a grip. You never sat on the cart with a load. That was not allowed unless on the hard road.

I remember once a horse slipping down and starting to kick as it lay between the shafts and we were instantly told to sit on its head. Then we were able to control it and we released the harness and got the horse up.

Its a long time since I saw a man on horseback driving a herd of 20 or more beasts through the village with only the help of his dog. This was a weekly scene when Henry Pask took Mr Deacon's cattle to Leicester Cattle Market from the Kilby area where Deacon had a large farm. Another scene was the Autumn sheep fair, where huge flocks of sheep were driven freely from the cattle market along the road to their new owners.

One interesting feature was the first appearance of a farm tractor, this was on the "Gravel Hills", two meadows in Newton Lane opposite the allotments. It was in the Spring of 1915 when these grass meadows were first ploughed for arable land. I am told that this tractor caused a sensation and was visited by many to see what was the beginning of mechanisation on Wigston farms.

Charlie Debreaux lived near Highgate. He was an old railway waggoner who had an allotment up Newton Lane. He told us how to make veal, just one of his many tales. When he was a lad he went down to the old slaughterhouses and a poor cow would come in and be killed immediately. A foot or hand pump would be put into the cow's body and some lads would pump vigorously whilst others hit the carcass with flat iron bars. The combination would tenderise the meat and raise the blebs which are so familiar with veal.

He told me the tale of the horse which jumped sideways every time he called out "Whoa!" The horse had been used to shunting, jumping out of the way to allow the trucks to roll by. This horse was hardly suitable for town work, as it kept jumping on to the causie (pavement) when "whoa" was shouted and knocking folks over!

We had a horse from Ellis' that when we started off with it, "jumped" into its collar, bang and stopped. We couldn't understand it, Charlie said that this was the trouble with having a "townee" horse. It was used to giving an almighty surge and the cart rolling behind it, but when it is on a field a country horse has to have its shoulders in the collar all the while because of the drag of the soil".

The Wigston laundry used to have some very good "vanners". Farmers used to consider it quite a catch if they could purchase one of them. Although they were no longer good enough for the laundry work, they were still adequate for farm work.

Soon after I had started work, I had to be like everyone else and wear leggings. An old boy stopped me and said, "Son, I hope you don't mind me telling you, but are your leggings catching on the harness of the horse as you jump on?". "Yes" I said, "they are rather". "Well he said, you have got them on the wrong way, you should have them with the flap of the leggings on the outside of your leg, then the muck won't get in and you don't catch it on the harness". The old dress had some finesse, although when leggings became shorter we liked the old gaiters which the Army were dishing out at that time. We even cut the feet off old gum boots and pulled the legs of the wellingtons over the boot to act as leggings.

Horse-drawn and motor vans at the Wigston Laundry, 1920s.

Another rare sight was Mr Walter Mason's high stepped horse and trap passing through the village. His wife was also a first class driver of these high steppers and competed in the London horse trials. A well known farmer besides his cattle business in Cook's Lane, his "Highfield" farm in Newton Lane was the show place of the village.

I learnt my work basically with horses, but when I had my first tractor I remember Vin Wilford's look of concern because he was losing a customer. The memory of my first attempt at ploughing with a tractor is vivid. John Copson was showing me how to operate the trailer plough and he said "Stop", I immediately shouted "Whoa!". Of course the tractor did not understand and the foot brake had to be used.

Jack Bailey, who at that time was farming Lodge Farm, had an old horse dray. He removed the shafts and fitted a draw bar to fit his old Fordson tractor. This had iron front and back wheels with great spikes on them. To travel on the road bands were put on these spikes so that they could move without ripping the road up. When the first pneumatic tyres were introduced, people put rubber tyres on the back wheels, but left the front iron wheel with a ridge or a rim round the middle of it so that they were only running on a two inch band, although the wheel itself would be four or five inches wide.

Jack's tractor was very slow. Low geared ones had a top speed of only about eight miles an hour. We found this rather laborious, so we often knocked it out of gear to coast down a hill. One snag though was that the clutch and brake were in one unit, and you had to put the clutch part-way down to disengage the gears and fully depress the rest to engage the brake. The brake was a transmission brake for use only at very low speeds as it had to brake on the fly wheel, so if you were at speed having notched out of gear and you tried to put the brake in, it caused a horrible screaming noise.

Jack Bailey decided that one of his old tipping carts would be better with rubber wheels. He managed to get a rubber wheeled axle and went to Ball's at North Kilworth to get them converted. He put the cart on the old dray and off he went. The dray still had on the old iron wheels. On the return journey George, Jack's son who was driving, got fed up with this slow and tedious progress so, at the top of Jane Ball hill he decided to knock the tractor out of gear. George went tearing down the hill overtaking cars!

Sitting on the dray was his father screaming blue murder – "Stop it George – stop it!", which George could not do. When he reached the bottom of the hill and slowed, father and son were both very shaken. It was a long time before George tried that dodge again!

SHEEP

I remember helping Norman Hill at lambing time in his yard where Kelmarsh Avenue is now. A lamb was being born by cesarean section. I held the ewe's back legs and was watching intently. I saw the heart of the sheep beating and suddenly I felt all woozy. The vet must have noticed because he shouted, "Put your head down boy, not enough time to look after the sheep without you", I came back to my senses and watched again with fascination whilst the sheep was sewn up. Mother and baby did satisfactorily after this.

The late Vin Wilford was one of the old type of country craftsman. He could plough a beautiful furrow and I learned a lot from working and listening to Vin who became a contractor in the village. Once, as a youth, he was bringing sheep from Kibworth through the crossroads on the Fleckney to Glen Road (which is the true Wistow Park, not the area on the Wigston side of the Hall which is the Nooks). It was not fenced off in those days to form the crossroads as we know it now and when he brought sheep through the gate, the sheep within the park immediately mixed in with his flock. He went home crying and told his sad tale to his father, who said "go back lad, you'll bring 'em out alright". When Vin got back there he found that the sheep had parted, his flock was grazing quietly on its own and the resident flock was doing likewise, and he brought his sheep home.

PIGS

I kept my first pigs on the allotments on Horsewell Lane. My allotment was just outside the Council field at the side of the old stream, fed from the horse wells from which the name of the lane was derived. I built two sties. I was 16 or 17 at the time and Frankie Woodward lent me some money to buy this allotment. In my spare time which was mainly at night, I used to fetch the bricks, sand and cement from Albert Lowe's yard in Bull Head Street, load them on my barrow and push it to where I was building my sties. The brickwork was uneven, but it did its job and I was so proud when eventually I took my own pig up to Freck's to be killed. I was taught how to take the "leaf" (fat) out and to render it down. I also learnt the art of curing bacon and ham.

When I kept pigs two natural medicines were used, one was iron sulphate purchased from the chemist. This was mixed with soil and placed in the creep adjoining the farrowing sow. At a day old the piglets would snuffle in and eat some. This prevented anaemia or the scours, which killed so many pigs. If older pigs were off colour or were bored and were biting each other, we would throw them some coal, the second natural medicine. Pigs loved to chew stones and push them about with their noses.

Ben Daetwyler, brother to my brother-in-law Max, was a great type. At the end of the war when "everything" was still short, Ben could get it, wire netting, gum boots, nails, you name it, in fact we said Ben was Chairman of Brum. Black Market! The only thing Ben was short of was pork, so a pig was purchased but no sty. Into the cellar it went and it thrived until mother asked for some coal to be brought up and they found that the pig had eaten the coal!

FARMING IN WARTIME

A favourite tale of Albert Palfry's was of the war years when a friend of his was involved in the black market. This friend (Joe) was a slaughterman and he did some black market slaughtering. He was in great demand because of the fact that he could also keep his mouth shut. He along with some others were caught red handed one day at his illegal trade. 'Bobby' Shred who went round to see him took great delight in saying, "Joe make great provisions, you won't be coming back for a while, we've got you this time".

Joe, having made provision, duly went to court. Who should be Chairman of the Magistrates, but one of Joe's bosses. The Magistrate was highly embarrassed, at the end of the hearing he said, "Joe we must stamp this out, prison is too good for the likes of you, you will only do your turn and come out, I am going to find you £500". Joe and his colleagues asked for time to pay, which was granted. Afterwards they told the Magistrate that if he didn't pay the fine for them they would make sure that he would go to jail with them. The group of employers had a whip round and handed the fine money over to one of Joe's colleagues, a man whose nickname was 'Long John'.

A few days later the bobby went to see Joe again, "Well he said, you got off with a fine Joe, but unless it is paid this week, you go inside!". Joe investigated and discovered that Long John had absconded with the money, so Joe and his colleagues had to go once again to their employers and say, "Pay up, or else" and their employers had to pay a second time. I believe this tale of Albert's, as I have also heard it from another source, which appears to corroborate the story.

Mr Freckingham had three sons and two daughters. The eldest son was named Eustace, who carried on the butchering tradition in the house and shop opposite the National School. His slaughter house was in operation during the war years when we killed pigs on licence. Obviously many tales, some true, some not so true, floated around about the slaughterhouse. It was said, tongue in cheek, that only heifer calves were born during the war, no steers or male calves, and rumour had it that males went to Freckingham's, or some other slaughterhouse, and then back to the farmer's kitchen! Since heifers became cows they couldn't be spared for slaughter.

Each family was allowed to have two pigs in a year. When pigs were taken along for slaughter the Ministry would purchase half from us if we did not want the whole pig. We always took the biggest and fattest pig we had for slaughter, but unless it was a monster the Freckinghams used to look down their noses and say, "Isn't it a waste killing that?"

The fatter the pig, the more "leaf" we could get out of the pig for rendering down to lard.

There are so many yarns about the black market! One involves William Evans who lived at Foston Lodge. Inspectors went round to see if he had got any blackmarket goods. William was not to be found, his sister was in bed. They apologised for disturbing her and searched around, but finding nothing came away. When they were clear of the farm gates, Evans who had been in hiding took the "bed" to bits and hung the bacon on the wall; sister had been lying on it. They had a tip-off one day that when they went to Wigston with the cart delivering their food, the police would be waiting and they would be caught. So they filled the cart with empty bottles and when the police searched them, the laugh was on the police. William Evans made a comfortable living but regrettably he eventually fell foul of the taxman and that was someone he could not beat.

One farmer told me how he sold a load of sheep in the war years. A lorry came, collected them and took them away. The payment was in cash of course. A couple of hours later the farmer happened to be going towards Leicester and was surprised when he overtook the same lorry. The next day he remonstrated with the driver for taking so long to get away from his farm, as he was fearful of being caught. He was told, "We were delivering the sheep!"

This surprised him but more surprises were in store when he found out that the lorry was a mobile slaughterhouse, with even a tray underneath to catch the blood!

The lambs were slaughtered and hung, as the vehicle travelled slowly round the country lanes. Being a cattle lorry it would not excite suspicion, by the time it reached the town, the lambs could be delivered, therefore, saving the storage problems and minimising risk of illegal slaughtering.

Vin Wilford one of our best village yarn spinners, told me about the time when he was ploughing with a caterpillar tractor and was trying to complete the ploughing of a field in the dark. He went over a bump, which he thought was an ant-hill. When he came round again he saw a dead sheep laying in front of him, he had run over it. He went to the farmer to apologise for killing his sheep. The farmer said, "Never mind lad, we can't be accused of being blackmarketeers when the sheep was killed accidentally, now can we?"

They had the sheep up and skinned it, and Vin had a joint for his trouble.

FOXES

One year Wigston had a real plague of foxes – lambs, pigs, cats and poultry were being taken. The hunt would not meet at Wigston because it is a "tight" area bounded by the railway and canal. A shoot was organised. Some 40 guns set off, firstly up the right hand side of the Newton Lane, the line stretching across to the railway line we walked to Newton. Then we walked the left hand side between Oadby and the Newton Lane up to Newton again. I believe there were 18 foxes shot dead that day apart from the wounded ones. Jumping over a stile early on I twisted my ankle and hobbled for the rest of the day.

Once I did shoot a fox. It jumped in the air, and everyone shouted "follow it lad, get it". Off I ran after it and coming round a corner I was confronted with the fox who turned its head sideways and snarled at me, I still have vivid memories of its brown teeth as it snarled. I shut my eyes and fired or I fired and shut my eyes. When I opened them the fox had gone and I was still trembling. The fox, as I learned from the men, always snaps at the side and not in front when it bites. Whether it was going to have a go at me I don't know. Having suffered severely from fox damage to my lambs, poultry, cats and young pigs, I have no sympathy or regard for the fox. I respect its cunning, but treat it as an enemy.

Lads used to catch foxes when they were cubs, dock their tails and then release them. As a fox tires it drops its tail, the tail becomes wet, drags and it gives the hounds a chance to catch him. Hounds could not catch docked foxes, to the great anger of the huntsmen.

Pop told us of an albino fox being caught at Knighton Spinney. It was bagged up and taken on show to Glen Parva Grange next to the Barracks at South Wigston. It escaped and literally ran through the pack of Fox Hounds and got away. Pop always said a fox had a better chance with the hounds than a man with a gun.

MY DOG RUFUS

A constant companion of my early farming days was my dog Rufus. Old Rufus was a cross between a shepherd Collie and something else. He was conceived on my allotment by a bitch I did not realise was on heat. What a wonderful accident that was.

One of Rufus's claim to fame was the fact that wherever I went he was with me and as I spent a lot of time on the tractor he would be on the

Myself with Rufus, 1950. Note the cobs of hay in the background.

trailer. As we built the load he would go up with it and stay on the top barking at people as we came back through the town. He was also the best ratter that walked the village. His most prodigious recorded feat was when we were threshing at St Wolstan's farmyard for Eric Hall. The dog packed off, Eric asked where the dog had gone, I said, "You look!" – the children had been there and they had laid out the kills. There was a line of some 90 rats that Rufus had killed and left, apart from the ones that he had eaten (he was rather partial to young baby rat).

When a stack of corn was threshed, by law wire netting had to be pegged around the stack some three to four feet away. The rats would jump out of the stack and be baffled by the wire then the dog would pounce. After many kills, Rufus would go home because he was sick of them. I ought to have washed his mouth out and given him a drink, but this was a dodge I was told later by the old threshing teamster Ralph Goddard.

One day whilst I was fetching hay from the cemetery there appeared a funeral cortege. I stood respectfully back out of the way, suddenly my dog Rufus gave a yelp and off he went, he had set up a hare, the hare went straight through the cortege followed by Rufus and I crouched behind a tombstone hoping that no-one would connect me with the dog. Some days later old Jack Bailey who was a mourner for this was his mother's funeral, said to me "Duncan that were your dog won't it?" and I shamefacedly admitted that it was. "Don't worry lad a dog would chase a hare, they don't worry about funerals, life still goes on in the midst of death".

He lived to be a ripe old age, but in the end sex killed Rufus. This sounds like the start of a corny joke on this subject, but Rufus was blind in one eye, and one dark and rather stormy night was knocked down by a car driven by an American stationed at Bruntingthorpe. The car had hit him on his blind side. The driver, who was very upset, came and reported the accident to me.

But why was he blind in one eye? The reason was that Gardner's dog from Upper Farm, Spa Lane, was his arch enemy and had many a fight over bitches. During one of these battles Rufus got blinded in one of his eyes. Ironically, whilst Rufus and Gardner's dog were fighting, a little spaniel had slipped in and attended to the desires of the bitch!

A Final Word

I hope these yarns, recollections and character sketches not only amuse, but also give some flavour of the rich character of life in Wigston earlier this century. Many reminiscences could not be included for lack of space, and perhaps one day another book can be produced. Until that day it is important that everyone tries to write down their memories of Wigston, or indeed any other community which has undergone marked change.

Many of the stories recorded here relate to tools, toys, pictures and lots of other artefacts. I have also tried to preserve as many of these as possible, and they are now on display in my private museum on Newton Lane, Wigston Magna. I am always interested in giving a good home to any other relics of Wigston's past.